DRAGNET

A Play in Three Acts

by James Reach

Based on the Famous NBC Radio-Television Series.
This adaptation has been authorized by Sherry TV, Inc.

A SAMUEL FRENCH ACTING EDITION

FOUNDED 1830
New York Hollywood London Toronto
SAMUELFRENCH.COM

Copyright © 1956 by Sherry TV, Inc.

ALL RIGHTS RESERVED

CAUTION: Professionals and amateurs are hereby warned that *DRAGNET* is subject to a Licensing Fee. It is fully protected under the copyright laws of the United States of America, the British Commonwealth, including Canada, and all other countries of the Copyright Union. All rights, including professional, amateur, motion picture, recitation, lecturing, public reading, radio broadcasting, television and the rights of translation into foreign languages are strictly reserved. In its present form the play is dedicated to the reading public only.

The amateur live stage performance rights to *DRAGNET* are controlled exclusively by Samuel French, Inc., and licensing arrangements and performance licenses must be secured well in advance of presentation. PLEASE NOTE that amateur Licensing Fees are set upon application in accordance with your producing circumstances. When applying for a licensing quotation and a performance license please give us the number of performances intended, dates of production, your seating capacity and admission fee. Licensing Fees are payable one week before the opening performance of the play to Samuel French, Inc., at 45 W. 25th Street, New York, NY 10010.

Licensing Fee of the required amount must be paid whether the play is presented for charity or gain and whether or not admission is charged.

Stock licensing fees quoted upon application to Samuel French, Inc.

For all other rights than those stipulated above, apply to: Samuel French, Inc.

Particular emphasis is laid on the question of amateur or professional readings, permission and terms for which must be secured in writing from Samuel French, Inc.

Copying from this book in whole or in part is strictly forbidden by law, and the right of performance is not transferable.

Whenever the play is produced the following notice must appear on all programs, printing and advertising for the play: "Produced by special arrangement with Samuel French, Inc., and Sherry TV, Inc."

Due authorship credit must be given on all programs, printing and advertising for the play.

No one shall commit or authorize any act or omission by which the copyright of, or the right to copyright, this play may be impaired.
No one shall make any changes in this play for the purpose of production.
Publication of this play does not imply availability for performance. Both amateurs and professionals considering a production are strongly advised in their own interests to apply to Samuel French, Inc., for written permission before starting rehearsals, advertising, or booking a theatre.
No part of this book may be reproduced, stored in a retrieval system, or transmitted in any form, by any means, now known or yet to be invented, including mechanical, electronic, photocopying, recording, videotaping, or otherwise, without the prior written permission of the publisher.

ISBN 978-0-573-60823-0   Printed in U.S.A.   #6111

DRAGNET

PROPERTY PLOT

ACT ONE

Scene 1

Dial phone
Pencils
Writing materials
Paper bag, 2 containers coffee, sweet rolls (Frank)
Coins (Joe)

Scenes 2 and 3

Telephone
Potted plant
Vases, ashtrays, bric-a-brac
Pocket knife (Joe)
Flashlight (Frank)
Notebook, pencil (Joe)
Book (Mrs. Gaylor)
Wristwatch (Frank)
Siren (*off Right*)

ACT TWO

Scene 1

Paperback book (Ray)
2 envelopes, cartridges (Ray)
Photographs

Scene 2

Paper, pencil (Tess)
Key (Joe)
Cartridge (Frank)
Newspaper
Cleaner (Nora)
Slip of paper (Frank)
Handcuffs (Frank)
Automatic pistol (Brad)

ACT THREE

Scene 1

Tray, coffee cups (Ginny)
Key (Joe)
File card (Frank)
Pistol

Scene 2

2 containers
Slip of paper (Joe)
Coins (Joe)

DRAGNET

CHARACTERS

(5 males; 5 females)

(In the Order in Which They Speak)

> Sergeant Joe Friday
> Officer Frank Smith
> Nora Hamlin
> Brad Roney
> Ginny Hamlin
> Mrs. Jessie Gaylor
> Walter Markov
> Dolores Shannon
> Ray Pinker
> Tess Brentwood

SYNOPSIS OF SCENES

The action takes place in a small office at Police Headquarters in Los Angeles; and in the living room of the Hamlin home.

ACT ONE

Scene 1

The office at HQ; the present; about 11:15 P. M.

Scene 2

The Hamlin living room; shortly afterward.

SYNOPSIS OF SCENES

Scene 3

The Hamlin living room; about five the following afternoon.

ACT TWO

Scene 1

The office at HQ; shortly afterward.

Scene 2

The Hamlin living room; later that evening.

ACT THREE

Scene 1

The Hamlin living room; about one hour later.

Scene 2

The office at HQ. About a month later. Late evening.

DESCRIPTION OF CHARACTERS

Joe Friday: About thirty. Has poise, a lithe strength, and a manner of quiet authority. His speech is clipped and terse and is usually read deadpan. Beneath his hard-boiled exterior, however, are qualities of sentiment and emotional involvement that only rarely show through.

Frank Smith: A few years older than Joe, built on a different pattern, and with a higher-pitched speech, to make a good foil for Joe. However, he has the same outward lack of emotions as he performs his job.

Brad Roney: In his late twenties. A brawny type, virile and athletic looking. Inarticulate and not well educated. There is a bitter brooding quality just below the surface that is always threatening to explode.

Nora Hamlin: In her early forties. Still quite handsome though slightly faded. Has the patient, stoic quality of a woman who has experienced much unhappiness.

Ginny Hamlin: About twenty-one. Has a great deal of charm; a capable self-reliant girl. Fiery and impetuous, not the type to consider consequences before acting.

Mrs. Gaylor: Seventy-three. A slight, shrunken figure. Has retained most of her faculties intact, although we get the impression that she views recent events through something of a haze.

Walter Markov: In his late forties. His appearance is unprepossessing, and his speech slow and heavy with a Slavic intonation. A man with deep emotions, which he finds difficult to mask.

DESCRIPTION OF CHARACTERS

Dolores Shannon: About thirty. A curvaceous blonde of flashy appearance. She gravitates naturally toward men, and her manner is cheap and tawdry.

Ray Pinker: In his late twenties. A slight and bespectacled young man with a studious appearance.

Tess Brentwood: In her early thirties. A small, intense woman with a dynamic manner and eccentric dress.

DRAGNET

THE SETTING

The playing area is divided into two units. At the Right, about two-thirds of the way across, and extending up about two-thirds of the depth of the stage, is a small office. The door to the office is midway in the Right wall. There is no window. A flat-top desk is placed down Left Center. There is a swivel chair back of the desk, and a straight chair to the Right of it. On the desk are a dial telephone, pencils and writing materials, etc. Against the Right wall, below the door, are several steel file cabinets. In the corner up Left is a coat rack. Other furnishings as desired.

The remainder of the width of the stage is set up as a living room. There are two entrances: A large arch in the back wall at the Right; and a door to the study about three-quarters of the way up in the Right wall. The arch leads, on the Right, to the front door of the house; on the Left, against the backing, is a stairway to the upper floor, the first few steps visible from the auditorium; below the steps to the Left is a hall leading to the kitchen and back of the house. Midway in the Left wall is a fireplace, with mantel above it. The windows are in the Left wall, upstage and downstage of the fireplace. Two loveseats at Left Center, forming a "V" and facing the fireplace; a low coffee table in front of the loveseats. A table for the telephone against the back wall, just Left of arch; a straight chair Left of table. An oblong library table against the Right wall, below the study door; a comfortable armchair downstage of the table. In the corner up Left, a large potted plant. In the corner down Left, a hassock or stool. Floor and table lamps, pictures, vases, ashtrays, and mantel bric-a-brac as desired.

When the action is taking place in one unit, the other unit is left dark. If desired, and if available, part-width drops, made of scrim or other diaphanous material, may be used to mask that portion of the stage not being utilized. These, however, are not necessary.

Dragnet

ACT ONE

Scene 1

The Time: *The present; Tuesday, March 24th; about 11:15. P.M.*

The Place: *The office in Police Headquarters.*

Before Rise: *The house lights dim and we hear* Joe's *voice over a microphone:* "It was Tuesday, March 24th. It was windy in Los Angeles. We were working the night watch out of Homicide Detail. My partner's Frank Smith. The boss is Captain Lohrman. My name's Friday. I'm a cop. It was quiet. You don't often get a breathing spell in my business, but tonight nobody was shooting at anyone. Maybe they'd sworn off for Lent. I was catching up on my reports."

At Rise: *The office area is lit up; the living room area is dark.* Joe *is discovered seated behind the desk working on a report. After a few moments,* Frank *enters with a paper bag in which are two containers of coffee and two wrapped sweet rolls. He hangs his hat up on the rack and comes down to* Joe.

Frank. Anything?
Joe. (*Not looking up from his report, shakes his head*) Huh-uh.
Frank. (*Removing contents from the bag*) Awful quiet tonight.
Joe. Yeah.

FRANK. Too quiet to last. Prob'ly start bustin' loose any time now.

JOE. (*Still immersed in his report*) Uh-huh.

FRANK. (*Pushing a coffee container and one of the sweet rolls toward* JOE) All out of jelly doughnuts. Cheese bun okay?

JOE. Yeah, fine. Thanks.

FRANK. (*Sits Right of desk, opens his coffee container and gulps from it.* JOE *has still not looked up*) Better take five, Joe. Coffee won't keep hot all night.

JOE. Just finishing. Like to have this report on the Skipper's desk when he comes in— (*After a moment, pushes the report aside, picks up the coffee container and leans back.*) How much I owe ya for this, Frank?

FRANK. (*Shrugs*) Forget it. You paid last night.

JOE. No, I didn't.

FRANK. Then ya can pay tomorrow night.

JOE. (*Shakes his head*) You need it more than I do, expenses you've had lately. How much?

FRANK. (*Hesitates, then gives in*) Thirty-seven cents. Odd pennies are for tax.

JOE. Right. (*Gets some coins from pocket, counts out the amount and pushes it across the desk to* FRANK) There you are. Pay for laundering your kid's diapers.

FRANK. Yeah, thanks. (*They eat and drink.*) I called home while I was downstairs.

JOE. How is it?

FRANK. Okay—now.

JOE. Kid over his croup?

FRANK. Yeah, got it licked at last. Doc was around this afternoon. Told Fay the little fella was in fine shape.

JOE. Good deal.

FRANK. She asked for you, Joe.

JOE. Fay did?

FRANK. Uh-huh— Wanted to know when you'd be comin' over to the house for a feed.

JOE. I'll make it one of these times.

FRANK. She said how about tomorrow evening?

ACT I — DRAGNET — 13

JOE. Wouldn't that be too soon?

FRANK. For what?

JOE. Might catch the kid's croup.

FRANK. If ya weren't a bachelor, you'd know better. You got a lot to learn about family life, Joe.

JOE. Maybe— But I guess I'll stay ignorant a while yet.

FRANK. (*Shoots him a look*) Aim to keep playin' it solo all your life?

JOE. (*Wryly*) Don't notice any gorgeous blondes battlin' to get their hands on me.

FRANK. They might if ya give 'em a chance.

JOE. (*Shrugs*) Why play 'em a dirty trick like that? I'm doin' okay as I am.

FRANK. Yeah— Better make it tomorrow for dinner, Joe. Fay's got a big roast in the refrigerator. Go bad if we don't cook it pretty soon.

JOE. Why don't you get her one of those freezers? Hear you can keep food a long time that way.

FRANK. Got any idea what they're askin' for freezers?

JOE. No. But you could buy it on time. Few dollars down and a little each month.

FRANK. Little each month here, little there. It adds up, Joe. To more than a cop's pay.

JOE. Yeah.

FRANK. (*Gulps coffee*) Maybe you got the right idea at that.

JOE. About what?

FRANK. Goin' it alone.

JOE. You think so?

FRANK. Always been somethin', ever since Fay and I got hitched. Trouble, I mean. Scroungin' to buy furniture, payin' for the little fella when he came. Sickness, bills, pills— Always somethin'.

JOE. Uh-huh.

FRANK. Sometimes it scares me, Joe.

JOE. That a fact?

FRANK. I swear to God, sometimes it does— Maybe you got the right idea.

JOE. (*Eyes him for a moment over top of coffee container*) Know what I think, Frank?
FRANK. What?
JOE. You're so scared, you're liable to die laughin'.

(FRANK *looks at him and breaks into a slow grin. The TELEPHONE rings.*)

FRANK. Well, here we go.
JOE. (*Reaching for the phone*) Yeah.
FRANK. Told ya it was too quiet to last.
JOE. (*Into phone*) Homicide, Friday— Yeah— Uh-huh— (*Gets pad and pencil from desk and makes notes.*) Hamlin— 2296 Whitworth Drive— Yeah, I'm gettin' it— Uh-huh— Uh-huh— Okay, we'll get right on it.
   (*Hangs up and tears slip from pad.* FRANK *looks at him inquiringly.*)
Suicide attempt—they think.
FRANK. Don't they know?
JOE. (*Shakes his head*) Fella locked himself into this room and they heard a gun go off inside. They can't get in.
FRANK. So they want us to.
JOE. Yeah. (*Rises.*) Better get movin'. Just in case the guy's still alive.
FRANK. Right.
   (*Rises and gets his hat from the rack,* JOE *picks up his hat from the desk and puts it on, then takes a final gulp from the coffee container.* FRANK *comes down near the door.*)
All set.
JOE. Yeah— (*Crossing to him.*) And Frank. This call, suicide attempt. See what I meant before?
FRANK. About what?
JOE. You thought you had troubles. (*As they turn to exit:*)

BLACKOUT

ACT ONE

Scene 2

THE TIME: *Shortly afterward.*

THE PLACE: *The Hamlin living room.*

AT RISE: *LIGHTS are up in the living room area; dark in the office area.* BRAD, GINNY *and* NORA *are discovered.* NORA *is ushering* JOE *and* FRANK *in.*

NORA. Right in this way. You from the police?
JOE. Yes, ma'am. This is Frank Smith. My name's Friday.
NORA. He's in there. (*Nods toward study door.*)
JOE. Who's "he"?
NORA. Karl Hamlin.
JOE. You his wife?
NORA. (*Hesitates a moment*) Nora Hamlin, yes. But we've been separated— He didn't live here.
JOE. (*Looking toward* GINNY *and* BRAD) Do they?
NORA. That's my daughter Ginny—Virginia. She lives here. The young man is Brad Roney, her friend. Manages the filling station on the corner.
JOE. (*As* BRAD *and* GINNY *nod tentatively, tosses them a little salute.*) Hi.
FRANK. (*Has crossed to study door Right during the above and tried the door*) Door's locked.
JOE. (*To* NORA) What's inside?
NORA. Kind of den—a study— You know. Full of Karl's books and things. I never moved them after he left.
JOE. Yes, ma'am. And you're sure he's in there now?
NORA. (*Nods*) He locked himself in—with his gun. (*Averts her look.*) Said he was going to kill himself.
JOE. (*Looks at her for a moment*) You didn't believe him?

NORA. (*Shakes her head*) Not till I heard the shot— Can't you do something? He may be hurt, suffering.

JOE. (*Crosses to study door and knocks on it*) Hamlin— Hamlin, can you hear me?

FRANK. (*After a moment*) Wanna try forcing it?

JOE. Guess we'll have to.

(*He and* FRANK *put their shoulders to the door and strain against it.*)

FRANK. (*After several unsuccessful attempts*) Isn't gonna give.

BRAD. Could've told you if ya asked me. You'll need an axe.

JOE. (*To* NORA) There another key to this door somewhere?

NORA. (*Shakes her head*) Only one we had was always left in the lock inside.

JOE. And there's no other way into the room?

NORA. No, this is the only door.

FRANK. How about windows?

NORA. What?

FRANK. Any windows opening into it?

NORA. Why—yes. Off the front porch.

JOE. Wanta try it, Frank?

FRANK. Okay. (*Turns to exit.*)

NORA. (*Stopping him*) There's screens— You'll need something to cut 'em with.

JOE. Here y'are. (*Gets out a pocket knife and hands it to* FRANK.) Bring your flash with ya?

FRANK. Yeah. (*Gets out a pocket flash, then exits through arch and off to Right.*)

JOE. (*To* GINNY *and* BRAD) You people hear the shot too?

GINNY. No, we—

BRAD. (*Topping her*) We weren't here when it happened.

JOE. That right?

BRAD. We had a date. Took in the show—
GINNY. The one over on Vermont.
BRAD. Good double feature. Westerns. One of 'em with John Wayne. I go for him.
JOE. Uh-huh.
BRAD. Then we stopped at the drugstore for a drink on the way back home—

(*The SOUND of a window pane being smashed is heard from off Right.*)

JOE. (*To* NORA, *as she starts nervously*) Sorry, ma'am. Guess he had to break the window to get in.
NORA. It's all right. Long as he gets to Karl in a hurry.
BRAD. (*Continuing his account to* JOE) Show was kinda long. Didn't get back till a few minutes before you arrived.
JOE. Uh-huh—

(*A KEY is heard turning in the lock, then the study door is opened from inside and* FRANK *appears.*)

FRANK. No wonder we couldn't force the door—
   (NORA *brushes past him and exits into study. He moves a heavy chair out of the way.*)
Had this chair propped up under the knob. And the door locked and bolted.
JOE. Yeah. Guess he really wanted to be alone— How is he?
FRANK. (*Shrugs*) Way you'd expect.
JOE. I'll take a look. (*Exits through study door.*)
GINNY. (*To* FRANK) He's dead, isn't he?
FRANK. Yes, ma'am.
BRAD. So he did it— Really went through with it. (*Shakes his head wonderingly as he sits on hassock down Left.*) Never thought he had the guts.
NORA. (*Re-enters from study, looking blank; in a dull*

voice) Well, he's gone— (*Crosses mechanically and sits in upstage loveseat.*) Karl is gone.

GINNY. (*Sits with her and tries to comfort her*) It'll be all right, Mom. Everything's gonna be all right.

NORA. (*Bleakly*) Sure. It's gonna be fine.

JOE. (*Re-enters from study and crosses to* GINNY) Coupla things I've gotta ask about your father, Miss.

GINNY. Go ahead.

JOE. (*Gets out a notebook and pencil*) You wanta give me his full name?

GINNY. Karl Lawrence Hamlin.

JOE. (*Taking notes*) Age?

GINNY. Forty-three.

JOE. Occupation?

GINNY. Nothing much, lately. Odd jobs once in a while—when he was sober.

JOE. Uh-huh. Where was he staying?

GINNY. Had a furnished room over on Bronson. Nine-forty-seven. Landlady's name is Miller.

JOE. Okay, thanks. (*Looks around.*) All right to use your phone?

GINNY. Of course.

JOE. (*To* FRANK) Wanta finish up in there while I start the wheels turning?

FRANK. Right.

(*Exits into study;* JOE *goes to the phone, picks it up and dials a number.*)

NORA. (*At same time*) Twenty years, and it had to end like this. I must've been somehow to blame.

GINNY. You weren't, Mom. You did everything. Everything a human being could—

JOE. (*Into phone*) Friday, Homicide. Better send a crew to 2296 Whitworth. Name's Hamlin— Right— Chest wound. Self-inflicted, looks like. Thirty-eight revolver— We're still checking, but it looks like suicide. Yes— Right. Good-bye. (*Hangs up phone and comes down to back of loveseat.*) Sorry, Mrs. Hamlin. I'll have to ask you a few questions.

NORA. All right, but—I'm not feeling too good. If you could make it short.

JOE. Yes, ma'am. Would you like us to call a doctor?

NORA. I've already called him. For my mother. He was out on another call. Said he'd be here in an hour or so.

JOE. Your mother lives here with you?

NORA. (*Nods*) She's in her room upstairs. Lying down. This whole thing's been a shock to her.

JOE. Uh-huh.

NORA. You gonna have to question her, too?

JOE. Yes, ma'am. We'll try to be as brief as we can.

NORA. I'd appreciate that. More than I can tell you. Terrible shock to her. She's not too well, anyway. In her seventies. You know how it is with people that old.

JOE. Yes, ma'am. Wanta tell me what happened now, Mrs. Hamlin?

NORA. Might as well get it over with. (*Takes a deep breath.*) Karl came over again tonight. Drunk. Made a scene.

JOE. It wasn't the first time?

NORA. (*Her eyes downcast*) No—

GINNY. It's been going on for three years, ever since they separated. Lately it was getting worse.

JOE. Uh-huh. Who was here at the time?

NORA. Just my mother and myself. Ginny had a date with Brad.

BRAD. We went to the movie. Then the drugstore on the way home. Like I told you.

JOE. (*Looks at him a moment*) Yeah— What time did Hamlin get here?

NORA. (*Promptly*) Little after ten-forty-five.

JOE. (*Taking notes*) Kinda late for a call, wasn't it?

NORA. (*Nods*) Yes, matter of fact I thought he wasn't gonna make it after all.

JOE. You were expecting him?

NORA. He called me at work this afternoon. Said he had

to see me. Had it worked out so that we could get back together again—

JOE. Yes, ma'am.

NORA. He'd kept calling me a lot. Been asking for a reconciliation. Saying how sorry he was and wanting me to take him back. Most of the time he was drunk.

JOE. Uh-huh.

NORA. I'm not blaming it all on him. I know some of it was my fault as well. (*Blows her nose.*)

JOE. (*After a moment*) Wanta go on, Mrs. Hamlin?

NORA. When he called this afternoon, I told him not to bother coming over. Wouldn't be any use— Not till he swore off drinking. For good.

JOE. Yes, ma'am.

NORA. But he insisted— Then tonight, it got late, and I started to go up to bed after the ten-thirty news. Way I usually do— There was a banging on the door. I went out and it was Karl.

JOE. Then what?

NORA. He was staggering. Eyes real glassy and all. 'Bout as bad as I'd ever seen him. I told him I wasn't gonna talk to him as long as he was in that condition. I left him here and went up to my room.

JOE. Was he alone?

NORA. No. Mother was still downstairs. She was going to stay up and read awhile. Doesn't sleep so much any more. You know how it is at that age.

JOE. Yes, ma'am.

NORA. Next I knew, I heard the shot—

JOE. How long after you went upstairs?

NORA. Not long. Fifteen minutes or so.

JOE. (*Taking notes*) That would make it about eleven?

NORA. (*Considers*) Little later. Eleven-ten, maybe.

JOE. Go ahead.

NORA. Well, when I heard the shot, I got back into my dress and came right downstairs.

JOE. What did you find?

NORA. Mother was standing in front of that door. She told me Karl was inside. That he'd shot himself.
JOE. Uh-huh.
NORA. I wouldn't believe it at first. I tried to get inside. Called to him to unlock the door. I thought he was only pretending, to arouse my sympathy. You know what I mean?
JOE. I think so.
NORA. But he didn't answer. It was awfully quiet in the study. And Mother said she'd heard him falling after the shot— I called you right away—

(FRANK *enters from study.*)

JOE. (*Takes a step toward him*) Find anything?
FRANK. I checked the gun. One shot fired.
JOE. Anything else?
FRANK. Doesn't look like it. No suicide note.
JOE. Fits with what Mrs. Hamlin's been telling me. He wouldn't have had time to write one.
FRANK. Uh-huh. Crew on their way?
JOE. Yeah— Maybe a coupla things we can clear up before they get here.
(*Steps back to* NORA; FRANK *holds Up Right.*)
Mrs. Hamlin, did your mother tell you what happened after you went upstairs?
NORA. (*Hesitates*) In a way she did.
JOE. What d'you mean?
NORA. Thing like this isn't too easy to go through at her age. She wasn't very coherent about it.
JOE. I see— Wonder if it'd be possible to talk to her.
NORA. Now? You have to?
JOE. (*Hesitates, then nods*) Afraid so, ma'am. After that, we'll have it just about finished.
NORA. All right. If it has to be that way.
GINNY. I'll call her, Mom! (*Rises, exits through arch and up the stairs.*)
FRANK. Joe.
JOE. (*Turns to him*) Yeah?

FRANK. That window I busted to get in the study—Ya s'pose there was any way of lockin' it from the *outside?*
JOE. (*Looks at him thoughtfully*) What d'you think?
FRANK. Maybe I better take another look.
JOE. Okay, go ahead.

(FRANK *exits through arch and off to Right.*)

BRAD. That's a fool idea. Nobody'd wanna lock a window from the outside.
JOE. That right?
GINNY. (*Runs downstairs and in through arch*) She's coming right down.
JOE. Fine. Thanks.
BRAD. You need me 'round here for anything, Sergeant?
JOE. (*Looks at him, then shakes his head*) No, I guess not.
BRAD. (*Rises*) Gettin' late and I'm on early shift in the mornin'. Hope everything turns out okay, Mrs. Hamlin.
NORA. Thank you, Brad.
BRAD. I'll buzz ya tomorrow, Ginny, and see what gives.
GINNY. Wait. Mom, I'm gonna walk a little way with Brad. I wouldn't be able to sleep anyway.
NORA. Well—don't stay too late, baby.
GINNY. I won't.
BRAD. So long.

(GINNY *takes his arm and they exit through arch and off to Right.*)

JOE. (*Watches them off, then to* NORA) You've got a fine-looking daughter, Mrs. Hamlin.
NORA. (*Nods*) Been a big help to me since Karl and I— Don't know what I'd have done without her.
JOE. Yes, ma'am. She engaged to Roney?

NORA. (*Decisively*) No!—Well, I mean you wouldn't call it exactly engaged. I hope not.

JOE. Don't think so much of him, eh?

NORA. (*Hesitates*) Oh, Brad's all right, I guess. In his way. Outside of that nasty temper of his. But a filling station attendant. Ginny's a smart girl. She could do better.

JOE. Uh-huh. Prob'ly could—

NORA. (*As* MRS. GAYLOR *appears on stairs*) Here's Mother. (*Rises and crosses through arch.*) I'll help you. (*Guides* MRS. GAYLOR *to armchair down Right and seats her.*)

MRS. GAYLOR. Thank you, Nora. (*She is clutching a book under her arm; carries this book on every appearance.*)

NORA. This gentleman is Sergeant Friday, of the police. He wants to ask you a few questions.

(JOE *crosses to them.*)

My mother, Mrs. Gaylor.

MRS. GAYLOR. How d'you do?

JOE. H'lo there, Mrs. Gaylor—I'll try to make this as brief as possible. Just a coupla little points you can help us clear up.

NORA. If you get tired, Mother, you tell him and he'll stop.

MRS. GAYLOR. It's all right, Nora. I'm perfectly all right now.

(NORA *looks at her doubtfully for a moment, then she crosses and sits on hassock Down Left to watch the scene.*)

JOE. (*Standing Left of* MRS. GAYLOR) I'm trying to find out what happened while your son-in-law was here. After your daughter went upstairs.

MRS. GAYLOR. Well, lemme try and think—I was sittin' right here in this chair. Might've dozed off for a minute—

Joe. Asleep?

Mrs. Gaylor. (*Shakes her head*) No, sir. Just dozin'— I can't sleep regular any more. Few minutes here and a few there. All I ever get.

Joe. Yes, ma'am.

Mrs. Gaylor. Well, Mr. Hamlin woke me up with his yellin'. Shouted he was gonna have a showdown with me—

Joe. (*With raised eyebrows*) With you, ma'am?

Mrs. Gaylor. That's what he said. Told me the split-up was my fault.

Nora. He was always claiming that. 'Course, there wasn't any truth in it. Just an excuse to save his own pride.

Joe. Uh-huh.

Nora. Mother didn't have a thing to do with our breaking up. If Karl had stayed sober, stopped running around, there might've been a way— But he wouldn't.

Joe. Yeah.

(*Looks at* Mrs. Gaylor; *her eyes are closed, chin on her chest. Sharply.*)

Mrs. Gaylor!

Mrs. Gaylor. (*Starts*) Yes, yes. I'm listenin'. Heard everything was said.

Joe. What happened after Mr. Hamlin started yelling?

Mrs. Gaylor. Why—I just sat here letting him rant— Till he began to curse at me.

Joe. He do that?

Mrs. Gaylor. I'm seventy-three, Mr. Friday. Been through a lot in my time—awful lot. But there isn't anyone I'll let talk to me like that. I told Mr. Hamlin. Told him to get out of the house— That's when he pulled this gun out of his pocket.

Joe. I see.

Mrs. Gaylor. Had it right in his coat. Outside pocket.

Joe. Uh-huh.

Mrs. Gaylor. I told him—I said—"Mr. Hamlin," I

said to him, "Now you stop this dang foolishness right now and clear out of here—Out."—That's what I said to him.

JOE. Yes, ma'am.

MRS. GAYLOR. He just looked at me and said, "You'd like that, wouldn't you?" Those are the exact words.

JOE. What did he mean by that?

MRS. GAYLOR. (*Shrugs*) You'd have to ask him, Mr. Friday. But that's what he said— Then he told me he was gonna kill himself. To show Nora and me.

JOE. Uh-huh.

MRS. GAYLOR. I thought it was just his dramatics. Mr. Hamlin was that kind. Always play-acting, trying to impress people. Know what I mean?

JOE. I think so.

MRS. GAYLOR. Wasn't play-acting this time— Next thing I knew, he ran into the study and locked the door—

JOE. That's when you heard the shot?

MRS. GAYLOR. Well, not right off— Few minutes later.

JOE. What happened during those few minutes? (*As* MRS. GAYLOR *doesn't answer.*) You doze again, Mrs. Gaylor?

MRS. GAYLOR. Could've. Not saying I did and not saying I didn't. I just don't remember.

JOE. Uh-huh.

MRS. GAYLOR. But I remember the shot, all right. And hearing Mr. Hamlin fall to the floor in there— That's when Nora came runnin' downstairs.

JOE. (*Finishing up with his notes*) All right, Mrs. Gaylor. Think I've got all the information I'll need.

MRS. GAYLOR. (*Seems disappointed*) You don't want to hear any more?

JOE. (*Shakes his head*) Don't think it'll be necessary.

NORA. (*Rises and crosses to her*) C'mon, Mother. I'll help you to your room.

MRS. GAYLOR. (*As* NORA *helps her to her feet*) You don't have to. I'm no invalid, y'know.

NORA. (*Crossing to arch with her*) I'll see you up. Better take a coupla those pills Dr. Bixley prescribed last visit. Maybe they'll help you sleep some.

MRS. GAYLOR. I doubt it, Nora. (*At arch, turns to* JOE.) Anything more you want to know about Mr. Hamlin—I'll be glad to tell you.

JOE. I'll let you know if there is. G'night, Mrs. Gaylor.

MRS. GAYLOR. (*Slowly going upstairs with* NORA) Goodnight, young man. Hope it will be for you— 'Twon't for me— (*They are off.*)

(JOE *walks slowly to Left, flipping the pages of his notebook*)

FRANK. (*Enters from Right and comes down through arch*) How's it look?

JOE. Huh? Oh— Seems cut-and-dried, Frank.

FRANK. Get all the statements?

JOE. (*Nods*) All checks out pretty straight— That is, if there was no way of locking that window from outside.

FRANK. (*Shakes his head decisively*) Wasn't. Less the guy's name was Houdini or something.

JOE. That's it, then. Nothing more to do but wait for the crew—

(*The DOORBELL rings.*)

FRANK. (*Exchanges glances with* JOE) Front door, isn't it?

JOE. Think so.

FRANK. Probably the crew.

JOE. Uh-huh—I'll let 'em in. (*Crosses through arch and off to Right.*)

WALTER. (*Off Right*) Who are you? What are you doing here?

JOE. (*Off Right*) Police officers. Who'd you wanta see?

WALTER. (*Off Right; agitated*) Police? What's the matter? What happened?

NORA. (*Hurrying downstairs*) It's Walter Markov. It's all right, Sergeant; you can let him in.

WALTER. (*Enters from Right*) Nora—
(*She goes to him and they come a few steps through the arch.* JOE *holds back of them.* FRANK *gives stage to Down Left.*)
What is it? What is happening here? (*Looks from* JOE *to* FRANK.) What do these men want with you?

NORA. They're from the police— About Karl.

WALTER. (*Looks at her searchingly*) Karl? He had an accident?

NORA. (*Hesitates*) He's dead. Shot himself.

WALTER. Shot himself— Dead— (*He doesn't seem very surprised.*) I—I'm sorry, Nora. This is a terrible thing should happen. For you.

NORA. I'll be all right.

JOE. (*Comes Down Right of* WALTER. NORA *is standing to Left of him*) Friend of the family, Mrs. Hamlin?

NORA. Oh— Pardon me for not introducing you, Sergeant. This is Walter Markov, my boss—

WALTER. (*Breaking in*) I'm her friend, too.

NORA. This is Sergeant Friday. And— (*Looks questioningly to* FRANK.)

FRANK. Officer Smith.

WALTER. (*Formally*) I am very happy to make your acquaintance.

JOE. Thanks. Mrs. Hamlin works for you?

WALTER. (*Nods*) Nora is my cashier. I run the Little Roumania Cafe, on Fountain Avenue. You know the place maybe?

JOE. (*Shakes his head*) Don't believe so.

WALTER. (*Gets a business card from his pocket and hands it to* JOE) Here is a card. Drop around sometime. I guarantee you will not leave hungry.

JOE. Okay, maybe I will— D-you know *Mr.* Hamlin, too?

WALTER. (*Hesitates, glancing at* NORA *before replying*) I knew him. He was a no-good— I'm sorry, Nora, but the truth is the truth. From him, Nora had nothing but heartaches. Believe me, nothing— A regular first-class no-good.

JOE. I wouldn't know. We never met.

FRANK. Mr. Markov, you make a habit of callin' on people at— (*Glances at wristwatch.*) Twenty minutes after twelve?

WALTER. No, sir. I was driving past, on my way home. I saw the lights on, a strange car in the driveway. So I wondered, maybe something is wrong.

FRANK. Uh-huh.

WALTER. (*Turns to* NORA, *looking at her feelingly*) Nora. Such a thing you should have to go through. I do not envy you. Tst, tst! (*Clucks sympathetically.*)

NORA. Hasn't been too bad. Everyone's been so kind to me.

WALTER. And such a surprise to me when you told me. A shock. (*A side glance to* JOE *to see if this is registering.*)

NORA. Guess it was to all of us.

WALTER. Nora, you shall not come in tomorrow. Take a few days off.

NORA. Who'll take cash?

WALTER. We'll manage. You will need a little time to get over this terrible—

(*A SIREN is heard off Right, fading in from a distance and getting louder during the following.*)

FRANK. Here comes the Crew.

JOE. Yeah. Mrs. Hamlin, if you don't mind. One more question before they get here.

NORA. I don't mind.

JOE. Your husband ever mention suicide? Before tonight, I mean?

NORA. (*Sighs*) Yes. Often. I never paid much attention. Just took it for granted it was the liquor talkin'. I didn't think he was serious. Never did.

ACT I — DRAGNET — 29

JOE. You had it wrong.
NORA. What?
JOE. He was this time—

BLACKOUT

ACT ONE

SCENE 3

THE TIME: *About five the following afternoon.*

THE PLACE: *The Hamlin living room.*

BEFORE RISE: *We hear* JOE'S *voice over a microphone: "12:24 A. M. The photographers got to the house and took pictures of the study, position of the body, and the Coroner took the remains to the County Morgue. 1:57 A. M. Frank and I left the house. We went back to the office and filled out the 3 point 11 point 1 form, listing the death of Karl Lawrence Hamlin as a suicide. Frank called the Coroner's office to find out when we could get the results of the autopsy. He was told they'd have the necessary information late that afternoon. 2:48 A. M. we signed out of the office and went home—At 3:59 P. M. we were back at the city hall. 4:29 P. M. The Coroner's office called, confirming the cause of death as suicide. At 4:40 Frank and I got to the Hamlin house."*

AT RISE: *LIGHTS are on in the living room area; off in the office area.* BRAD, GINNY *and* MRS. GAYLOR *are discovered.* MRS. GAYLOR *is in the armchair Down Right, the book clutched in her hand, her eyes closed, chin on chest. The DOORBELL rings.* GINNY *goes to door, opens it and we see* FRANK *and* JOE *enter the room.*

JOE. (*Off*) Afternoon, Miss Hamlin.
FRANK. (*Off*) Afternoon. Your mother in?
GINNY. (*Off Right*) Yes, she is. Come in, please.
(*Re-enters, followed by* JOE *and* FRANK. BRAD *gives stage, crossing to fireplace.*)
I'll tell her you're here. (*Turns and exits up the stairs.*)
JOE. (*Taking a few steps through arch with* FRANK) Afternoon, folks.

(BRAD *looks at them, then deliberately turns his back, crosses Down Left and sits on hassock.*)

MRS. GAYLOR. I remember you. You're the detectives.
JOE. Yes, ma'am.
MRS. GAYLOR. You come to get some more information about Mr. Hamlin?
JOE. (*Shakes his head, smiling*) No, ma'am. That won't be necessary now.
FRANK. This's just a routine call.
MRS. GAYLOR. (*Disappointed*) Oh! Mean it's all over?
FRANK. Uh-huh. 'Cept for a few formalities.
JOE. How you feeling this afternoon, Mrs. Gaylor?
MRS. GAYLOR. Well as I ever do. It'd be fine. Just fine—if I could only sleep. Awful hard to do without it.
JOE. (*Deadpan*) Yes, ma'am. It must be.
NORA. (*Enters downstairs and through arch, followed by* GINNY. *She is dressed in mourning black. Comes down to* FRANK *and* JOE *while* GINNY *crosses and sits in upstage loveseat*) Goood afternoon.
(JOE *and* FRANK *ad lib greetings.*)
Sorry to keep you waiting. I was up in my room. Haven't been feeling too good.
JOE. Hope it's nothing serious.
NORA. (*Shakes her head*) Just a nervous headache. It'll pass after I— Is this call about—?
JOE. Yes, ma'am. Thought you'd wanta know the results of the Coroner's investigation.
NORA. What were they?

ACT I DRAGNET 31

Joe. Been confirmed as suicide—
Brad. What d'ya mean, "confirmed"? Wasn't ever any question, was there?
Joe. (*Looks at him without replying; to* Nora) Thought you'd wanta know, Mrs. Hamlin.
Nora. Yes. Thank you. And what—what do I do now?
Joe. About—Mr. Hamlin, you mean?
 (Nora *nods.*)
Apply to the County Morgue. They'll help you make the arrangements.
Nora. There won't be any trouble about it?
Joe. No, ma'am. None at all.
Ginny. Mom. You're not going to— Not planning on—?
Nora. (*Sighs*) Someone has to bury him, Ginny.
Ginny. But why you?
Nora. Isn't anyone else.
Ginny. Let him go to the Potters field. You don't owe him anything. And he didn't leave any insurance, did he?
Nora. (*Shakes her head*) He let his policy lapse years ago.
Ginny. Let the County worry about burying him. You don't owe him a thing, Mom.
Nora. You're wrong, Ginny. This much I owe him.
Ginny. For what?
Nora. (*Hesitates, smiling wryly*) For you— For almost twenty years, a few of 'em not so bad— For a number of things you couldn't understand, baby. You're too young yet. Maybe some day you will—
Joe. (*After a moment*) That about wraps it up, far as we're concerned.

(*The DOORBELL rings.*)

Nora. Excuse me. I'll see who that is. (*Crosses through arch and exits to Right. Off Right.*) Oh—It's you, Dolores.

DOLORES. (*Off Right*) H'lo, Nora. Is that a police car in the driveway?

NORA. (*Off Right*) Yes. They're inside now.

DOLORES. (*Off Right*) Could I see them a minute?

NORA. (*Off Right. Reluctance in her voice*) Why— Yes, guess you can— C'mon in.

(*Re-enters with* DOLORES; *latter is wearing a scanty sun suit.*)

DOLORES. Nora, I wanta tell you how much I sympathize with you in your tragic— (*Stops short, looking around.*) Oh— Pardon me. Why didn't you tell me you had such a full house?

NORA. Guess there's always room for one more. (*Crosses to back of downstage loveseat.*)

DOLORES. (*Comes down between* JOE *and* FRANK, *who make room for her*) H'lo, Mrs. Gaylor—Ginny—Brad.

(*They ad-lib greetings. Looks down at herself.*)
Have to pardon my outfit. I was out back, trying to get a little sun. Gotta work fast these days. What with the smog and all.

JOE. You wanted to see us, ma'am?

DOLORES. If you're the police, I do.

JOE. Yes, ma'am. This is Officer Smith. I'm Sergeant Friday.

DOLORES. How d'you do? I'm Dolores Shannon. I live next door.

JOE. *Mrs.* Shannon?

DOLORES. (*Nods*) That's the name I use. Been divorced, though. 'Bout a year now.

JOE. Uh-huh.

DOLORES. You fellows investigating Karl Hamlin's death?

JOE. We were.

DOLORES. "Were"?

FRANK. Case's about closed now.

DOLORES. Oh? And you're satisfied it was suicide?

FRANK. Yes, ma'am.
JOE. Do you have any reason for thinking it might not be?
DOLORES. (*Hesitates*) Why— Yes. Matter of fact, I have. (*Nooks at* NORA.) You're gonna hate me for this, Nora. But— Every citizen's got an obligation. I mean when it comes to cooperating with the police— Isn't that right, Sergeant?
JOE. That's right, ma'am.
DOLORES. Last night. I heard something—
JOE. That right?
DOLORES. In this house. You know how these places are built.
JOE. Uh-huh.
DOLORES. And I'm right next door. Almost hear a paper rustling in here from my living room— And I— (*Looks at* NORA; *then defiantly.*) I felt it was my obligation to let you know. As a citizen.
JOE. Yes, ma'am. Just what'd you hear?
DOLORES. A number of things. I heard the shots, too. But before that, I heard—
JOE. Just a minute. You said "shots."
DOLORES. Well? There were two.
JOE. That right? Mrs. Hamlin, how many'd you hear?
NORA. One.
JOE. Mrs. Gaylor?
MRS. GAYLOR. (*Hesitates momentarily*) One.
FRANK. And only one was fired from Hamlin's revolver.
DOLORES. (*Adamantly*) I can't help that. I heard two.
FRANK. Both together?
DOLORES. No. Coupla seconds between them. Two or three.
JOE. What time was that?
DOLORES. (*Reflects*) Eleven. Or a little after.
BRAD. One of 'em could've been a backfire.
JOE. Yeah.
DOLORES. Anyway— That isn't what I was gonna tell you about.

JOE. All right. Go ahead.

DOLORES. This was earlier. Shortly after ten. I know, because I was expecting a phone call. From a gentleman who—a phone call— That's when I heard this fight.

JOE. Fight? In here?

DOLORES. That's right, Sergeant.

JOE. Who was fighting?

DOLORES. One of them was Karl Hamlin. And the other—

NORA. (*Has been reacting worriedly to* DOLORES' *story*) You must've been mistaken in the time, Dolores—

DOLORES. I wasn't.

NORA. But you must've been. Karl didn't get here till past ten-forty-five.

DOLORES. (*Coldly*) I don't want to contradict you, Nora. But I couldn't have been mistaken. I was expecting this call, and it was late coming. I kept looking at the time. It was a little after ten.

NORA. (*Shakes her head*) You must've got mixed up somehow. Karl didn't show up till after the ten-thirty news. I told you that, Sergeant.

JOE. Uh-huh. You told us. (*To* DOLORES.) About the fight. Who was the other party?

DOLORES. Another man.

JOE. D'you recognize his voice?

DOLORES. (*Hesitates*) No— But I'd heard it before. Here lately in this house. It was—sort of different.

JOE. Different, ma'am?

DOLORES. Uh-huh. Not the voice of—of an American. Know what I mean, Sergeant?

JOE. Yeah.

DOLORES. Kind of European. Maybe Hungarian. Roumanian— (*Glances at* JOE *to see if it's registering.*) Something like that.

JOE. Uh-huh. What about it, Mrs. Hamlin?

NORA. (*Shakes her head*) She must've heard Karl shouting at me. Or Mother. There wasn't any other man here. Not till—till afterwards.

DOLORES. Sorry, Nora. Didn't mean to get you in dutch or anything. But I felt it was my—
GINNY. (*Smiles coldly*) Your duty. We know, Dolores.
DOLORES. (*To* JOE) There were two men.
JOE. What were they fighting about?
DOLORES. Couldn't tell you that. But they sure were mad. Thought they'd tear each other apart, way they were goin' at it.
JOE. Hear anything else?
DOLORES. The shots. Then later, someone smashin' a pane of glass.
JOE. All right. Thanks for the information, Mrs. Shannon.
DOLORES. You're welcome, Sergeant. Though it wasn't easy. Barging in here like this and telling you.
JOE. Guess not.
DOLORES. Hope I've been some help— Nora, you do understand why I had to—?
GINNY. (*Scathingly*) We understand perfectly, Dolores.
DOLORES. (*To* JOE *and* FRANK) Anything else I can do for you, just call on me. I'm right next door. 2294.
JOE. We'll keep it in mind.
DOLORES. Good. (*Smiles from* JOE *to* FRANK.) 'Bye now. 'Bye, all. (*Nods curtly to* OTHERS, *turns and exits through arch and off to Right.*)
GINNY. (*Jumps up angrily*) That—cat!
BRAD. Sure showed her claws that time.
GINNY. The nerve of her. The barefaced nerve. Coming here—into this house—and spouting a pack of lies like that.
JOE. She have any reason for lying, Miss?
GINNY. Reason enough. She and my father—
NORA. (*Peremptorily*) Ginny!
GINNY. The Sergeant wanted to know her reason.
NORA. We don't have to go into that. Not now. It's over now. (*To* JOE.) It's over, isn't it, Mr. Friday? Got everything you need, haven't you?

JOE. (*Hesitates, then nods*) Guess we have, Mrs. Hamlin.

NORA. Let the dead past bury its dead. Decently— (*Turns away, holding a handkerchief to her eyes.*) Decently—

(*The PHONE rings.*)

MRS. GAYLOR. (*Has dozed off during the above; awakens with a start*) Telephone— Phone's ringing.

GINNY. I'll get it. (*Rises, crosses and answers phone.*) Hello— Yes, this is the Hamlin residence— That's right; did you want to speak to him?—Just a moment. (*Leaves phone on table and comes down.*) It's for you, Sergeant Friday.

JOE. Thanks. They say who it was?

GINNY. Yes, but I couldn't quite make out the name. Binker— Something like that.

FRANK. Ray Pinker from the Lab.

JOE. Yeah. (*Crosses and picks up phone.*) Friday— Yeah, Ray— Uh-huh, just getting ready to leave— That right? (*Listens deadpan.*) Uh-huh— Uh-huh— Uh-huh— Yeah, I get the picture— Okay, we'll make it down there soon as we can and take a look at it. Right.

(*Hangs up, then slowly turns and looks at them; the* OTHERS *stir uneasily.*)

FRANK. Somethin' up, Joe?

JOE. Yeah— Yeah, somethin's up— The case is open again.

NORA. Open? What do you mean?

JOE. Just that, ma'am. Call was from the Police Laboratory. They were making a routine check of the evidence. And they uncovered something— It rules out the possibility of suicide.

GINNY. You mean he didn't kill himself?

JOE. We don't think so.

GINNY. Then what happened?
JOE. Only one answer.
GINNY. What?
JOE. He was murdered.

BLACKOUT

END OF ACT ONE

ACT TWO

Scene 1

THE TIME: *The same evening; shortly afterward.*

THE PLACE: *The office at Police Headquarters.*

BEFORE RISE: JOE'S *voice is heard over a microphone:* "5:29 P. M. FRANK *and I went back to the office. We took the Freeway downtown and made pretty good time, arriving at the office at 5:47.* RAY PINKER *was waiting for us."*

AT RISE: *The LIGHTS are on in the office area; off in the living room area.* RAY *is discovered, seated behind the desk reading a paper-backed book. He is wearing a suit. After a moment,* JOE *and* FRANK *enter.*

JOE. Hi, Ray.
FRANK. (*As they cross in to desk*) How they goin'?
RAY. (*Intent in his reading*) Shhh. Don't interrupt. I'm right at the climax.
FRANK. Yeah?
RAY. (*Folds back a page and puts book aside*) Guess I'll have to finish it later—These guys are wonderful, y'know?
JOE. Who's that?
RAY. These private eyes. One man working alone, and he outsmarts the whole Police Department of a big city.
FRANK. Real genius, huh?
RAY. Wonderful brain. Brilliant— You fellas oughta take lessons from him.
JOE. Sure— When we get the time. What've you got for us, Ray?

RAY. I'll show you.
> (FRANK *and* JOE *come closer to him, one on either side, behind the desk.*)

I was running a routine check this afternoon, when it turned up.

FRANK. What?

RAY. Take a look— (*Opens an evidence envelope and shakes a cartridge into the palm of his hand.*) This is the bullet I fired from the gun you found in the victim's hand.

JOE. Yeah.

RAY. Weighs a hundred and thirty grams.

FRANK. What're you tryin' to prove?

RAY. (*Takes another evidence envelope and shakes a second cartridge into the palm of his hand*) This is the bullet that killed the man. (*Hands it to* JOE.) Take a look.

JOE. (*Examines it*) Outta shape.

RAY. See anything else there?

JOE. (*After a moment*) No— Looks all right to me.

FRANK. What're ya buildin', Ray?

RAY. I checked this one pretty carefully. Made sure that all of it was here. Y'know— That none of the lead had been sheared off by bone tissue.

FRANK. Uh-huh.

RAY. None missing. It's complete.

FRANK. So?

RAY. It weighs ninety-five grams.

JOE. Lighter than the other one.

RAY. Right. Thirty-five grams difference— Let me show you something else here— (*Holds both bullets up together.*) Notice the difference in length?

JOE. Yeah— Well, what's it mean, Ray?

RAY. (*Holds up one of the bullets*) This slug—the one that killed Hamlin—is a .380. European calibration.

FRANK. .380, huh?

RAY. (*Holds up the other bullet*) This one—from the gun you found in his hand—is for a .38 revolver.

FRANK. Yeah.

RAY. .380's automatic ammunition. Shell should've been ejected when Hamlin was killed. But you didn't find one last night.

FRANK. Wasn't any reason to look for it then. Not with that revolver in Hamlin's hand.

RAY. There's a reason now. (*Tosses bullets back onto desk.*) Way you had it, this fella Hamlin really pulled a neat trick.

JOE. What d'you mean?

RAY. Killed himself with a bullet that couldn't possibly have been fired from the gun he was holding.

FRANK. Something sure out of place.

RAY. Might as well tear up the forms you filled out on this one. It's no suicide.

JOE. (*Sighs*) Sure was a pretty case. Everything fit— Sometimes I wish they'd never invented science.

RAY. What you hafta do now is look for a .380. The murder gun.

JOE. Yeah—wait a minute, Ray— (*Frowning in thought.*) Maybe you can tell us how that gun—and the murderer—could've got in and out of a locked room.

RAY. (*Reflects*) Sure it was really locked? All around?

FRANK. Positive. Pictures the boys took'll bear that out.

RAY. I've got 'em right here. (*Picks up a set of photographs from desk.*)

JOE. Let's see now— (*Finds the right one.*) Here— Door locked, key on the inside. Then bolted. And a chair propped up under the knob.

RAY. Uh-huh— What's this broken window?

FRANK. I hadda break it. Only way to get into the room.

RAY. (*Looking at the picture*) Those walls plaster?

FRANK. Right, solid plaster. No chance of anyone gettin' through them.

RAY. How about the bookcases?

FRANK. What d'ya mean?

ACT II — DRAGNET

RAY. These bookcases here. Any of 'em pull away from the wall?

FRANK. (*Shakes his head*) Checked 'em last night. All seemed solid enough.

JOE. (*Smiles*) No false panels or secret passages there, Ray. Isn't that kind of a place.

RAY. Uh-huh.

JOE. Way it was set up, nobody could've shot him, then gone out, locked the door and propped that chair up inside.

RAY. Doesn't seem likely.

FRANK. (*Shakes his head*) Looks like we're really out there in left field.

JOE. Yeah— Unless Ray's got the answer.

RAY. Certainly I've got the answer.

FRANK. Ya have?

RAY. It's simple. Guy in that book I was reading would've come up with it in the first chapter.

JOE. Okay. We're listening.

RAY. All you've gotta do is look for a butler.

FRANK. Butler?

RAY. Yeah. One built like an envelope.

BLACKOUT

ACT TWO

SCENE 2

THE TIME: *Later that evening.*

THE PLACE: *The Hamlin living room.*

BEFORE RISE: JOE'S *voice is heard over a microphone: "6:16 P. M.* FRANK *and I headed back for the Hamlin house. We had a couple of things to look for, couple of people to talk to. The case was wide open again, and I had an unpleasant hunch it was going to stay that way for a while."*

AT RISE: *The LIGHTS are on in the living room area; off in the office area.* NORA *is discovered in the living room with* JOE *and* FRANK. GINNY *is also in the room.*

JOE. As far as you know, is there another gun in the house?
NORA. No, sir. I don't like them around.
JOE. Suppose someone might have a pistol and you wouldn't know about it?
NORA. I don't think that's likely.
JOE. (*Turning to* GINNY) How about you, Miss Hamlin?

(*Interrupting her speech we hear the DOORBELL ring.* NORA *rises and walks to the door. She opens it and we hear* TESS BRENTWOOD.)

TESS. (*Off Right*) Good evening. You're Mrs. Hamlin, aren't you?
NORA. (*Off Right*) That's right—
TESS. (*Off Right*) May I come in?
NORA. (*Off Right*) If you'll tell me what you want—
TESS. (*Off Right*) Of course, Mrs. Hamlin. Glad to. But we can't talk out here, can we? (*Enters.*)
NORA. (*Following her on; angrily*) Just a minute! You can't do that—
TESS. (*Looks around the room, sees* GINNY, JOE *and* FRANK) Joe Friday, boy sleuth. Looks like you're not gonna be able to use your finger-print kit.
JOE. Hello, Tess.
TESS. (*Looks back at* NORA) And you're the widow. The bereaved Nora. My deepest condolences.
NORA. (*Stares at her*) Who're you?

TESS. (*Shrugs carelessly*) Doesn't matter a lot. (*Sits on loveseat with* NORA.) I've come to help you.

NORA. Help me? How?

TESS. By letting the world know about you. Telling 'em what you've gone through. Getting them on your side.

NORA. (*Persistently*) Who are you? What's your name?

TESS. (*Smiles easily*) You do have a one-track mind, don't you, darling? You can call me Tess—

GINNY. (*Has been standing Right of them*) You're Tess Brentwood! Of the *Herald-Times*.

TESS. Give the little girl a big cigar.

NORA. (*Uneasily*) A reporter?

TESS. Definitely not, darling. Feature writer. There's a difference, believe me. Difference of ten years of pounding dusty pavements and a hundred dollars a week salary.

NORA. What do you want of me, Miss Brentwood?

TESS. I've come to do things for you. Big things. We're going to unleash the power of the press in your behalf— By the way, you *are* innocent, aren't you, darling?

NORA. What do you mean?

TESS. You didn't kill your husband, did you?

NORA. (*Gasps*) Me! Kill my—?

GINNY. Mom. I don't think you ought to talk to her.

NORA. I don't either— (*Looks at* TESS *uneasily*.) Is that what they're saying? That I—?

TESS. (*Shrugs*) They will be, probably. Dick Tracy, Jr., here will unless we can do something to forestall them fast.

GINNY. I don't think you ought to say anything, Mom—

TESS. (*Sharply*) Listen to me. Both of you. Flash came in a little while ago from the Police Press Officer. Every paper in town has it by now. And it looks like an interesting story. With gimmicks. Murder made to look like suicide—

NORA. You mean they're going to write about—*us*—in the papers?

TESS. (*Nods*) At length, darling. Been slow today—nothing much happening. That's the only crime item with any angles that's come through all day. It'll get a play, and nobody can stop it. Only question is, *how* do you want it played? From your viewpoint, or— (*Shrugs.*)

NORA. (*After a moment*) What do you want to know?

TESS. Good. Now we're being smart, darling. (*Pats her hand approvingly.*) Here's the way we'll work it. Our man on the police beat will get the facts. What I want is your story. (*Gets pencil and paper from her handbag.*)

NORA. *My* story?—I haven't got one

JOE. You've got plenty of time to stop the press, Tess. You don't mind if we get on with our business.

TESS. (*Paying no attention*) Of course you have— How long were you married to the brute?

NORA. Almost twenty years.

TESS. (*Making notes*) Separated?

NORA. About three.

TESS. Why'd you break up?

NORA. (*Shrugs*) Usual reasons, I s'pose.

TESS. He drank, didn't he?

NORA. (*Hesitates*) Some.

TESS. And ran around?

NORA. (*Troubled*) I— What good's it gonna do to print stuff like—?

TESS. (*Harshly*) Just a minute. You don't seem to have it straight yet, darling. You want people—your friends, neighbors, everybody—to think you're a murderer?

GINNY. (*Angrily*) That's ridiculous!

TESS. Is it? Okay. Let the crime boys write it their way and see how it turns out.

NORA. And you can— Can prevent them from—?

TESS. Of course. People believe what they read. If they see it in print, it's so.

NORA. Guess that's true.

TESS. We'll let 'em read about you. Long-suffering wife. Drunken beast of a husband. Made her life a hell on earth. But she took it all bravely, uncomplainingly. A good woman. Sweet, gentle. Obviously wouldn't harm a fly.

GINNY. Not exaggerating much there— Maybe Miss Brentwood has a point, Mom.

NORA. Maybe.

TESS. All right. (*Rises and walks around, sizing up the room.*) We'll want pictures. My cameraman's out in the car— (*Comes back to examine* NORA *carefully.*) Mmmm— You look all right— (*Looks at her through cupped hands, as through a picture frame.*) Stunned, grief-stricken widow. Yes. (*Turns to* GINNY.) Not bad— You'll need a black dress, darling. Preferably a low-cut one.

GINNY. (*Shakes her head*) You can leave me out of it.

JOE. You really haven't got any taste, have you?

TESS. I'd answer that one, Strongheart, but I can't reduce it to one syllable words. (*She turns to* GINNY.) Don't be silly, darling. Have to have something for the boys. You'll fill the bill beautifully— (*As* GINNY *starts to protest.*) For your poor dear mother's sake, of course—

JOE. All right, Tess. You just ran out of time. See you around the City Room, huh?

TESS. (*Shakes her head*) Sorry. Nora invited me in. She's giving me her story exclusively.

JOE. Maybe so but not on City time. See you around.

TESS. (*As she moves to front door*) You're gonna regret this, Hawkshaw. I get through with my story you're gonna look like a bum.

JOE. You've tried it before. You got one thing against you, Tess. Too many honest reporters in the business to let you look very good.

(TESS *gives him a disdainful look and leaves the scene.*)

NORA. (*After a pause*) She—she said she wanted to help me.

JOE. Kind of stuff she writes—sometimes it does more harm than good.

FRANK. They call her "Miss Slushbucket" 'round the City Rooms. Time she gets through writin' about ya, ya don't recognize yourself.

NORA. I wasn't gonna talk to her at first, but— According to her, people will say that I— That I killed Karl.

GINNY. Ridiculous of course. Isn't it, Sergeant?

JOE. (*Looks at her for a moment without replying, then to* NORA) Hafta ask you some more questions, ma'am.

NORA. (*Nods*) I was expecting that.

FRANK. (*Comes down*) Want me to try the study again for that casing?

JOE. Yeah. (*Gets a key from his pocket and hands it to him.*) Here's the key.

(*During the following,* FRANK *unlocks the padlock and exits through study door.*)

Mrs. Hamlin— That revolver your husband had.

NORA. Yes?

JOE. Where did he get it?

NORA. Couldn't tell you that. He had it for years.

JOE. That the only gun he had?

NORA. (*Nods*) Far as I know.

JOE. How about you?

NORA. What?

JOE. Any other firearms in the house?

NORA. No.

JOE. You pretty sure about that?

NORA. Yes. I—

GINNY. What makes you think there might be another one?

JOE. (*Disregarding her; to* NORA) How many shots did you hear last night, Mrs. Hamlin?

NORA. I told you this afternoon: just one.

JOE. But Mrs. Shannon next door heard two.

NORA. She was—mistaken.

JOE. (*Shakes his head*) No, ma'am. Two shots were fired.

NORA. How do you know that?

JOE. We know.

NORA. And what difference does it make how many were fired?

JOE. Makes quite a difference, ma'am. Difference between suicide and—murder.

FRANK. (*Re-enters from study; crossing to* JOE) Won't find it now. Room's been cleaned.

JOE. Did you clean the study, Mrs. Hamlin?

NORA. (*Nods*) This morning. With the rest of the house— Was there any reason I shouldn't have?

JOE. No, ma'am, not this morning there wasn't. You didn't find an empty shell casing?

NORA. Casing? I don't know what you mean.

FRANK. Like this. (*Gets a cartridge from his belt.*) This brass part of the bullet.

NORA. (*Shakes her head*) I didn't see anything like that.

JOE. What did you use to clean the room?

NORA. What d'you mean? I vacuumed, and—

JOE. Uh-huh. That vacuum—did you empty it since then?

NORA. (*Reflects*) Don't think so— No.

JOE. Wonder if we could see it?

NORA. (*Looks at him for a moment, then rises*) All right. I don't understand what this is all about, but if you want to see the vacuum, I'll get it. (*Crosses up to arch.*)

FRANK. Want me to give ya a hand with it?

NORA. You don't have to. It's right out here in the hall closet. I can manage— (*Exits Left below the stairs.*)

JOE. (*To* GINNY) Got some newspaper we could borrow, Miss?

GINNY. (*Looks around, then points to a folded newspaper on coffee table*) Right there, Sergeant.

Joe. Thanks. (*Gets it and spreads it out on floor Down Center.*)
Nora. (*From off Left*) You want the attachments, too?
Frank. No, ma'am— Just the cleaner itself.
Nora. (*Re-enters with cleaner*) Okay, here you are—
Frank. I'll take it. (*Gets it from her and brings it down to newspaper.*)
Joe. (*Looks it over*) This the way you get the dust bag out?
Nora. That's right— Just flip that catch on the side there.
Joe. Uh-huh.

(*Flips the catch and lifts the dust bag out. Nora and Ginny stand back of them watching curiously while Joe and Frank carefully sift dirt from the bag onto the open newspaper.*)

Frank. (*After a few moments*) Got something here that feels like— Yeah— Here it is. (*Straightens up, examining shell, then hands it to Joe.*) Take a look.
Joe. (*Looks it over*) Uh-huh.—.380 all right.

(*During the following, Frank carefully replaces the dirt in the bag and inserts it into cleaner, crumpling up the newspapers.*)

Nora. (*To Joe*) What's all that mean?
Joe. Means there were two shots fired here last night.
Nora. (*Carefully*) I—I really don't understand.
Joe. It's simple, ma'am. There was this one— And the one fired from your husband's revolver.
Nora. I—
   (*As Joe keeps looking at her steadily, she averts her gaze.*)
I only heard one— (*Turns away.*) Only one.
Joe. Uh-huh.
Nora. This— This whole thing is crazy. Just crazy.

ACT II　　　　　　　DRAGNET　　　　　　　　49

Joe. But the evidence makes it true.

Nora. Who'd want to kill him? And how could they do it? You saw the way the room was locked last night.

Joe. Yes, ma'am— But I also see this. (*Holds up the shell.*) This says Karl Hamlin was murdered.

Frank. (*To* Ginny) Wanna take these, Miss?

Ginny. (*Reluctantly; she has been watching* Nora *apprehensively*) All right. (*Takes the bunched-up newspaper and the cleaner from* Frank *and exits Left below the stairs.*)

Joe. Mrs. Hamlin— Don't you think it's about time now?

Nora. Time for what?

Joe. To tell us what really happened last night?

Nora. I've already told you.

Joe. Maybe you forgot something. Thought it might be coming back to you now.

Nora. (*Shakes her head adamantly*) No. I've told you everything that happened—everything that mattered.

Joe. How about the things that didn't?

Nora. (*Looks at him beseechingly*) Mr. Friday— Why do you have to dig like this into matters that don't concern you?

Joe. A man's been killed. It's up to us to find the person that did it. It's what we're paid for.

(*The DOORBELL rings.*)

Nora. Excuse me. (*Exits through arch and to Right. From off Right*) Oh—Walter.

Walter. (*Off Right*) Nora, you're all right. You are feeling all right now?

Nora. (*Off Right*) Yes, fine. The police are here again, but I guess you can come in.

(*Re-enters, followed by* Walter.)

WALTER. I won't stay long— (*To* JOE *and* FRANK.) Good evening, gentlemen.

(*They nod and ad-lib greetings.*)

NORA. (*Coming Down Center with him*) You shouldn't have done it, Walter. Shouldn't have left the restaurant during rush hour.

WALTER. (*Grimaces deprecatingly*) The restaurant. Who cares about business at a time like this? Besides, it was slow tonight. The girls could handle it.

(*Simultaneously,* JOE *has taken* FRANK'S *arm, dropped upstage with him and spoken to him sotto voce.*)

FRANK. (*Nods his understanding*) Right. I'll get on it. (*Turns and exits through arch and off to Right.*)

WALTER. (*Simultaneously to* NORA) So? It's all right now?

NORA. (*Hesitates*) I don't know.

WALTER. (*Looks at her with concern*) Nora— What is wrong?

NORA. I— The police think Karl was—murdered.

WALTER. (*Reacts strongly*) Murdered? No, no, it could not be. It's impossible.

NORA. That's what I tried to tell them.

WALTER. Last night suicide and tonight murder? This I never heard before.

NORA. That's what they say.

WALTER. Why? Why, Nora? It does not make sense. What gives them such an idea?

NORA. Seems there were two shots fired—

WALTER. Two?

NORA. (*Nods*) So they claim. One from his own revolver didn't kill him. And the other— (*Turns away distractedly.*) I don't know. I'm confused—

WALTER. (*Looks at her compassionately. Shyly puts a hand on her arm*) Nora. A thing like this, it should happen to someone else. Not you. A fine woman like you—I hate to see this.

NORA. (*Turns back to him gratefully; with a thin smile*) Thanks, Walter. And don't worry about me.

WALTER. Murder— (*Shakes his head and clicks worriedly.*) Tst-tst! Who? Who would do such a thing?

JOE. (*Has been taking it in from Up Center. Comes Down Right of* WALTER. NORA *is Left of him*) Maybe you can help us find out, Mr. Markov.

WALTER. (*Looks scared*) I? No, no. I know nothing. You understand, Mr. Detective? Nothing.

JOE. Sometimes people know more than they think they do.

WALTER. (*Keeps shaking his head*) I would be glad to help. But believe me, there is nothing I can tell you.

JOE. Then you won't mind answering a few questions.

WALTER. (*Carefully*) No, go ahead. But from me you will find out nothing. Believe me.

(GINNY *re-enters from Left. She stops short as she takes in the situation, then crosses and sits at telephone table watching.*)

JOE. You were here last night, weren't you?

WALTER. Last night? Of course. You saw yourself when I came, Mr. Detective. We talked about the Little Roumania. I gave you a card—

JOE. (*Shakes his head*) I mean before that.

WALTER. (*Wets his lips, looking worried*) Before?

JOE. While Karl Hamlin was still alive.

WALTER. (*Glances nervously at* NORA; *she frowns and shakes her head almost imperceptibly*) No! While Karl was alive, I was not here.

JOE. (*Looks at him quizzically*) Sure?

WALTER. Yes, yes. I am positive.

JOE. You didn't get here about ten, or a little later?

WALTER. No—

JOE. And you didn't quarrel with him?

WALTER. I, quarrel? With Karl?

JOE. (*Nods*) Yeah. Loud enough to be heard outside the house.

WALTER. (*With an attempt at a smile*) You could tell me why, maybe? Why I should have a quarrel with Karl Hamlin?

JOE. I was hoping you could tell me, Mr. Markov.

WALTER. (*Shakes his head*) How could I quarrel with him if I was not here?

JOE. That's what you claim?

WALTER. Of course. Ask Nora and she will substantiate this. Last night while Karl was alive, I was not here.

NORA. (*Readily*) That's right, Mr. Friday. He's telling you the truth.

JOE. (*After a moment*) You both willing to stand on that statement?

NORA. (*She and* WALTER *exchange glances*) Yes.

WALTER. I am willing to stand on it.

JOE. Okay. We'll hold things as they are for a coupla minutes. Till— (*Breaks off and listens;* FRANK *and* DOLORES *are heard off Right.*)

FRANK. (*Off Right*) Ya can go right in.

JOE. Now we'll see—

DOLORES. (*Enters from Right with* FRANK; *comes through arch and stops. She is wearing a clinging satin hostess gown*) Is it all right?

JOE. Yeah. Come in, Mrs. Shannon.

DOLORES. (*Comes down, giggling self-consciously.* FRANK *holds Up Right*) You'll have to pardon my appearance again. Officer caught me as I was dressing to go out. Hope you understand.

JOE. Uh-huh, we understand— Mrs. Shannon, d'you know Walter Markov?

WALTER. (*Bows formally*) I am happy to make your acquaintance.

DOLORES. Hello, there. Oh yes, I know him.

WALTER. (*Looks at her inquiringly*) I am sorry. I do not remember—

DOLORES. You run that restaurant, don't you? Little Roumania?

WALTER. Of course. This everyone knows.

DOLORES. Been in there a coupla times for dinner. Enjoyed the food a lot.

WALTER. I thank you.

JOE. (*To* DOLORES) Ever seen Mr. Markov here before? In this house?

DOLORES. (*Hesitates*) No— Haven't been in this house much—I mean inside it. Not lately.

JOE. Uh-huh. Mr. Markov, would you mind shouting?

WALTER. What? Shouting? I do not understand.

JOE. I want you to holler. 'Sif you were mad at someone.

WALTER. But— Why, Mr. Detective? Why you want I shall do this?

JOE. Just running a little experiment. 'Course, we can't force you to do it. If you don't wanta cooperate—

WALTER. (*Hesitates, thinking it over*) What shall I holler? What do you want me to say?

JOE. (*Shrugs*) Suit yourself.

WALTER. (*Raises his voice in feigned anger*) Come to the Little Roumania! Only the finest food and the best service! You will enjoy the experience! Open every night until twelve! (*In his normal voice.*) This is what you had in mind?

JOE. Yeah, thanks. How about it, Mrs. Shannon?

DOLORES. (*Nods*) He's the one I heard last night—

NORA. (*Fearfully*) Oh, no!

DOLORES. No question about it. Couldn't mistake that voice.

GINNY. (*Jumps up angrily and comes down*) Don't you realize, Sergeant?

JOE. Realize what, Miss?

GINNY. She's making this all up—

DOLORES. (*Bristles*) Listen! Are you intimating that I would—?

GINNY. I'm intimating nothing. I'm telling you to your face, Dolores: you're a liar.

DOLORES. Don't you dare! Don't you dare say a thing like that about—

GINNY. I'll say that and more. You're not only a liar—you're a cheat!

(*They are standing face to face; these lines are read fast and furiously.*)

DOLORES. Oh, is that so?

GINNY. Yes, that's so! I should think even you would have enough shame not to come into this house after what you—

DOLORES. Don't flatter yourself that I wanted to. I'm only here because the officer asked me to help with—

GINNY. You're a cheat and a wrecker. The way you kept running around with my father, encouraging him to drink—

NORA. (*With an ineffectual gesture toward her*) Ginny. Please. There's no need to rake up old—

GINNY. (*Speaking through her to* DOLORES) You did your best to break up this home—

DOLORES. I didn't have to break it up. That was done a long time ago. By your mother. She made life so miserable for that poor man, no wonder he drank—

GINNY. (*Looks at her scathingly*) Haven't you got any shame at all?

DOLORES. I'm only interested in one thing. Seeing justice done. That's why I'm here now—

GINNY. Justice! If justice were done, you'd be the first to—

DOLORES. (*Shrilly*) That's enough! I'm not gonna stand here and take any more of your insults.

GINNY. (*Tauntingly*) Didn't mean to hurt your pride, Dolores. I just didn't think you had any.

DOLORES. Why—why, you! (*Lunges for her.*) I'll teach you to—

JOE. (*Quickly gets between them*) Hey! Ladies. Hold it, will ya?

GINNY. Let her try. I wish she would.

NORA. Ginny. Baby. That's no way to act.

GINNY. I just couldn't take any more of her hypocrisy—

DOLORES. Talk about hypocrisy! The way you carry on at all hours with that cheap hoodlum from the filling station—

GINNY. What's the matter, Dolores? Sore because you couldn't get Brad for yourself? I know you tried. Too bad he's out of your league for class—

DOLORES. That's enough.

(*Straining to reach her as* JOE *keeps them apart.*) Let me at her— Just let me at her.

GINNY. Let her, Sergeant. Go ahead.

NORA. Ginny, stop it! Do you hear me—?

JOE. (*Holding them apart by main force*) Hold it now— Both of you! (*Pushes* DOLORES *away.*) Okay, Mrs. Shannon— Guess you've told us all we need for now. You can go.

FRANK. (*Comes down and takes* DOLORES' *arm*) C'mon, lady. I'll see ya to your door.

DOLORES. (*Stands glaring at* GINNY *for a moment, then permits herself to be led to the arch*) Okay. It'll be a pleasure to get out in the fresh air. (*Turns at arch.*) And I hope you get to the bottom of this fast, Sergeant. I hope they get just what's coming to them.

(FRANK *leads her out to Right.*)

GINNY. (*To* JOE) You're not going to take her word for anything?

JOE. Why shouldn't I?

GINNY. Couldn't you see? Couldn't you tell the type she is?

JOE. What type is that, Miss?

GINNY. If you want me to be absolutely blunt about it, a tramp.

NORA. Ginny!

GINNY. (*Heatedly to* JOE) She had her hooks in my father, all right. Don't know why she bothered. Except that he was a male. But he was only one. One of many.

JOE. Uh-huh.

GINNY. A crowd. That's the way she likes it. All kinds. And if you're looking for a murderer—

NORA. (*Firmly*) That's enough, Ginny. You're talking too much.

GINNY. I just want the Sergeant to know what she is.

JOE. Okay, Miss. You've told me. I know.

GINNY. I hope so.

JOE. But she still heard a fight in here last night. A quarrel. (*Turns to* WALTER.) What about it, Mr. Markov?

WALTER. (*Hesitates, sighing gloomily*) Nora— Maybe it would be better now that we shall tell him the truth.

NORA. But Walter—

WALTER. Sooner or later it will come out. It would be better they shall hear it from us.

NORA. (*Looks at him, then shrugs wearily*) All right. If you think so. (*Turns away to fireplace.*)

(GINNY *looks at her, crosses to her, and puts a hand on her arm reassuringly.*)

WALTER. (*Sits in armchair Down Right. Eyes downcast*) I was here last night. Karl also. We had a quarrel.

JOE. What time was it?

WALTER. (*Shrugs*) Who remembers? If you say a little after ten, I will take your word for it.

JOE. What was the quarrel about?

WALTER. It was about— (*Shoots a look at* NORA.) About Nora and me.

JOE. Uh-huh.

WALTER. You shall understand me, Mr. Detective.

Nora Hamlin is a fine woman. For three years she works for me—since the separation. I have learned to know her very well. A fine woman—

Joe. Yeah.

Walter. The best. And my intentions, you understand, were strictly honorable. So many times—so many times I asked her she should marry me.

Joe. That right?

Walter. But Nora, she would not. She put me off. This she will not admit, but she kept hoping. Always she was hoping that this no-good, this Karl, he would change, so she would be able to take him back.

Joe. Uh-huh.

Walter. A foolish hope. I tell her, I say, "Nora, could a leopard change its spots? Could a hog stop rolling around in the filth?" But she would not listen. Still she put me off—

Joe. And last night?

Walter. Last night? Last night I came here. Karl was here. He was stinking from whiskey. Blind.

Joe. Yeah.

Walter. He was cursing at Nora. Such things he was saying. Carrying on something awful. A disgrace. So naturally, I tried to make him stop it.

Joe. Uh-huh.

Walter. He turned on me. He accused me of—of terrible things I was doing with Nora. You understand?

Joe. (*Nods*) I think so.

Walter. This I could not take. About me I did not mind. But such things he should be saying about Nora— It is not often I am losing my head, Mr. Detective, but this time I lost it.

Joe. Uh-huh.

Walter. I jumped on him. I was so mad, I could— Believe me, if I could tear him apart with my two hands, last night I would have done it—

Joe. What happened after you jumped him?

Walter. Nothing.

JOE. (*Looks at him*) Nothing?

WALTER. Nora came between us. Karl was not responsible, she told me, for what he was saying. She begged me I should leave the house.

JOE. Then what?

WALTER. I left.

JOE. Just like that, huh?

WALTER. Yes, sir. For Nora's sake— Because she asked this.

JOE. Uh-huh. And when'd you come back?

WALTER. When? You saw when, Mr. Detective. You answered the door yourself. You let me in.

JOE. (*After a moment*) Mrs. Hamlin?

NORA. (*Turns to him*) Yes?

JOE. You got anything to say?

NORA. Walter's told you the truth. The complete truth.

JOE. That's what you said before.

NORA. This time it's true.

JOE. Whyn't you tell us so in the first place?

NORA. (*Hesitates*) I didn't want Walter involved. Didn't see any reason for it. That fight between him and Karl. Accusations Karl made in his drunkenness. Didn't see why our dirty linen should be washed in public when there was no reason.

JOE. Uh-huh. So you called Mr. Markov and told him to say he hadn't been here earlier?

NORA. Yes.

JOE. When? What time'd you call him?

NORA. Right after Karl— After I put in the call for you.

JOE. You tell him that Hamlin had shot himself?

NORA. (*Hesitates momentarily*) Yes.

JOE. (*To* WALTER) So you knew before you got here? The second time?

WALTER. I knew.

JOE. (*To* NORA) Okay. There was the quarrel and you got Mr. Markov to leave. What happened then?

NORA. I've already told you.

JOE. Tell me again.

NORA. (*Marshaling her thoughts*) Why—Karl kept ranting at me. I told him I wasn't gonna listen to him as long as he was in that condition. I went upstairs.

JOE. What time was it then?

NORA. Ten-forty-five. I remember looking at my watch and thinking Karl had made me miss the ten-thirty news.

JOE. You went up and left your mother down here with Hamlin?

NORA. Yes. She was nodding in her chair.

JOE. She'd been here all the time?

NORA. No. She came down right after Walter left. She'd been upstairs trying to sleep. Said she couldn't.

JOE. Uh-huh. Then you went upstairs and a little later you heard the shots.

NORA. Yes. After fifteen, twenty minutes. Something like that. Only—there was just one shot.

JOE. You still claiming that?

NORA. (*Earnestly*) I only heard one, Mr. Friday. It's the truth. You've got to believe that.

JOE. (*Looks at her for a moment, then starts pacing, frowning in thought; comes back to her*) Someone else might've come in here while you were upstairs.

NORA. Someone else? Why—I s'pose they might have.

JOE. Your mother would know if they did.

NORA. No! I mean—not necessarily. She dozes a lot. You've seen the way she is. Half the time, she doesn't know what's going on.

JOE. We can check with her and find out.

NORA. I wish you wouldn't, Mr. Friday.

JOE. Why not?

NORA. She told you everything she knows. Last night.

JOE. (*Skeptically*) So'd you, ma'am. Remember?

NORA. She wouldn't lie to you. Not Mother. Wish you didn't have to disturb her now. She's asleep.

JOE. How d'you know?

NORA. I made her take two sleeping pills. Right after supper. She didn't want to, but I made her— Whatever you have to ask her, Mr. Friday, couldn't it wait?

(JOE *looks at her, hesitating.*)

BRAD. (*Enters from Right and through arch*) Hi! Door was off the latch.
GINNY. Oh—Brad. (*Takes a step toward him.*)
BRAD. How they goin', honey?
GINNY. (*Frowns*) I—I don't know.
BRAD. (*To* JOE) You guys still at it?
JOE. Yeah, still at it.
BRAD. (*With a cold grin*) Reg'lar little ole bulldogs, aren't ya?
JOE. (*Smiles back at him*) Hope you never feel our bite, friend.
BRAD. Don't worry about me. I can take care of myself.
JOE. Sure.
BRAD. (*To* GINNY) Haven't forgotten our date, have ya?
GINNY. No, but—I don't think I ought to go.
BRAD. Why not?
GINNY. I just don't think I ought to leave. Not now.
BRAD. Aw c'mon, honey. Don't be like that. Can't carry the weight of the whole world on those little shoulders of yours.
NORA. Brad's right. Why don't you go, Ginny? It'll do you good to get away from the house.
GINNY. (*Shakes her head*) I wouldn't feel right about it, Mom—Brad, I'm sorry, but I don't think I'd better—
FRANK. (*Enters from Right. Stops inside arch Up Right*) Oh, Joe.
JOE. Yeah?

(FRANK *motions to him and he crosses up.*)

FRANK. I called back in from Mrs. Shannon's place. To see if they had anything for us.
JOE. Did they?
FRANK. Yeah— Yeah, they had somethin', all right.
JOE. What?

FRANK. Know that check we put through with R and I?

JOE. (*Nods*) Blanket check on everyone concerned, yeah.

FRANK. Here's what they came up with. (*Gets a slip of paper from his pocket and hands it to* JOE.)

JOE. (*Looks at it carefully*) Uh-huh— Yeah, I get the picture.

BRAD. (*Has been taking this in uneasily*) Well— If you're sure you don't wanna come along, honey, maybe I'd better mosey. (*Turns and takes a few steps up.*)

JOE. Maybe you'd better not.

BRAD. (*Stops, eyeing* FRANK *and* JOE *tensely*) What d'ya mean?

JOE. (*Steps in closer to him*) Wanta talk to you—now that we know about your record.

BRAD. (*Angrily*) *Record?* What're ya talkin' about? I got no—

JOE. Better not make any rash statements. We've got your Parole report right here— (*Reads from paper in his hand.*) "Subject, Bradley J. Roney—" That's you, isn't it?

(BRAD *looks sullen, refuses to reply.*)

"Arrested June, 1951, in Los Angeles County after a street brawl—Victim succumbed to stab wounds—Subject was convicted of manslaughter and sentenced to state penitentiary at Chino, four to ten years—Released and placed on parole last November after serving 32 months—"

GINNY. (*Looks at him unbelievingly*) Brad—Brad, is it—true?

BRAD. (*Bitterly*) Yeah, it's true. Now ya know all about it.

GINNY. Why did you keep it from me? You should've told me.

BRAD. And have you give me the heave as a stir bum? Ya'd've liked that, wouldn't you?

JOE. Doesn't always work out that way, Roney.

BRAD. (*Flaring*) Whatta you know about it? You're a

cop, ain't ya? You boys know only one thing: how to sink the screws in a guy. Bunch o' holier-than-thou hypocrites, every one of—

JOE. Easy. Better take it easy.

BRAD. (*Shrilly*) *Easy?* First ya wreck my life, then ya tell me to take it easy. I got a good mind to— (*Suddenly lashes out, swinging wildly at* JOE.)

JOE. (*Ducks the punch*) Cut it out now—

GINNY. (*As* BRAD *lunges again at* JOE) Brad, don't— please don't!

(FRANK *comes down to lend a hand as* BRAD *swings at* JOE *again.* JOE *ducks inside the punch and lands two hard punches on* BRAD'S *stomach. The latter sinks to the floor on one knee, grimacing with pain.*)

FRANK. If ya insist on playin' rough, son, we'll have to do this— (*Gets his handcuffs out and slips them over* BRAD'S *wrists.*) Now get on your feet. (*Pulls* BRAD *up and starts to frisk him.*)

BRAD. (*Looks at* JOE *with deep hatred*) Okay— Okay, we'll finish this some other time— Don't think it's over just because you got in a lucky punch—

FRANK. (*Frisking* BRAD, *suddenly pulls up one of latter's trouser legs, uncovering an automatic pistol strapped to the calf of* BRAD'S *leg.* GINNY *gasps as* FRANK *gets the pistol and examines it. Turns to* JOE) Take a look. (*Hands him the pistol.*)

JOE. Yeah— English make— A .380. (*To* BRAD.) Wanta tell us about this?

BRAD. (*Sullenly*) Figure it out for yourself.

JOE. Won't be hard. A .380 killed Karl Hamlin— What it figures out to is that you're in this thing— Awfully deep.

BLACKOUT

END OF ACT TWO

ACT THREE

Scene 1

THE TIME: *About one hour later.*

THE PLACE: *The Hamlin living room.*

BEFORE RISE: *We hear* JOE'S *voice over a microphone:* "8:05 P. M. FRANK SMITH *went back to the office and I stayed with* BRAD RONEY *at the Hamlin house —We weren't ready to book* RONEY *yet. We wanted to give him every chance to tell us the truth. Ballistics was running a test on his gun to see if it matched the slug that had killed* KARL HAMLIN. *But* RONEY *wasn't being very cooperative. We sat around the living room, waiting—"*

AT RISE: *LIGHTS on the living room area; off in the office area.* JOE, BRAD *and* NORA *are discovered.* BRAD, *still in the handcuffs, is seated in the armchair Down Right, slouched back in the chair, his expression blank.* NORA *watches restlessly from upstage loveseat.* JOE *is seated on the hassock Down Left.*

GINNY. (*The above tableau holds for a few moments, then we hear her voice from off Left*) Coffee's ready— (*Enters from Left, below the stairs, carrying a tray on which are several cups of coffee. Crosses to loveseat.*) Mom?
NORA. Thanks. (*Takes a cup from tray.*)
GINNY. (*Comes down to* JOE) Sergeant?
JOE. Thanks a lot, Miss. (*Takes a cup.*) Appreciate it.
GINNY. That's all right. (*Starts to cross to* BRAD *and*

stops short.) Oh— (*Turns back to* JOE.) Sergeant, couldn't you take those things off? Just while he has his coffee?

JOE. (*To* BRAD) Promise to behave yourself if I take 'em off?

GINNY. (*After* BRAD *refuses to answer*) He'll behave. I promise for him. (JOE *looks at her for a moment, then puts his cup down on the floor beside him, rises and crosses to* BRAD, *gets out a key, unlocks and removes the handcuffs.*) Thank you, Sergeant.

JOE. Uh-huh. (*Crosses, sits on hassock again and picks up the cup.*)

GINNY. (*At same time, crosses to* BRAD *with the tray*) Go ahead, Brad. (*He looks up at her.*) I poured one for you— No sense wasting it.

BRAD. (*Takes a cup from the tray*) Okay— Might as well give ya the satisfaction if ya wanna make like a do-gooder. A bleedin' heart—

GINNY. (*Starts to reply angrily, then changes her mind*) I— Do you have to talk like that?

BRAD. (*Shrugs*) What's it matter to you? Ya don't have to soil your fingers on the likes of me. Not any more.

(GINNY *looks at* BRAD, *then sighs, puts tray down on the coffee table, takes a cup and sits on downstage loveseat.*)

JOE. (*After a moment, to* BRAD) Now that you started talkin', feel like keeping it up?

BRAD. Doesn't make a lot of difference if I talk or not, does it?

JOE. Depends. On what you say. Might make a whole lot of difference— Difference of your life, for instance.

BRAD. (*Laughs bitterly*) That's a good one— Ya got me now. Found out about my record. Caught me violatin' parole and packin' a rod. Isn't that enough for ya?

JOE. (*Shakes his head.*) Not quite.

BRAD. What more d'ya want, for Pete's sake?

JOE. To listen to your side of it. Your statement—

BRAD. Statement? Okay, I'll give ya a statement: Go jump in the lake. You and all like ya.

JOE. (*Looks at him and shrugs*) If that's the way you want it.

BRAD. Yeah. That's exactly the way.

GINNY. (*Looks at* BRAD *appraisingly, then turns to* JOE) Sergeant— Would you let me try?

JOE. Huh? Try what?

GINNY. I think he might talk to me.

JOE. Sure. Go ahead.

GINNY. I mean alone.

JOE. (*Looks at her*) I'm afraid we can't do that.

NORA. You go ahead and talk. I don't think he's got anything to say that I want to hear.

(*She leaves the room.* JOE *settles back a little away from the couple.*)

BRAD. (*To* GINNY) What're you gonna try and get me to say?

GINNY. Brad— Don't you see? Don't you realize that my only concern is to help you?

BRAD. I don't care for your brand of help.

GINNY. Listen—I'm going to stand by you, no matter what—

BRAD. (*Sarcastically*) Oh, sure.

GINNY. I'm going to stand by you. If they arrest you for killing my father, I'll get a lawyer. The best.

BRAD. They come high. You'd be wastin' your dough.

GINNY. What d'you mean?

BRAD. They hafta make an arrest. That's all they're interested in. And I'm elected. They got a pretty good case against me.

GINNY. No matter how good a case they've got against you, if you didn't do it, they can't—

(BRAD *is looking at her searchingly.*)

What's the matter, Brad? Why are you looking at me like that?

BRAD. That's not what ya really think.

GINNY. What isn't?

BRAD. That I didn't do it. Didn't knock off your old man.

GINNY. Of *course* that's what I really think.

BRAD. Don't try to hand me that.

GINNY. Listen— If I didn't think so, would I be standing here right now? Talking to you like this?

BRAD. Right along you thought I was the one—
   (*She shakes her head.*)
Don't deny it. Since we had that squabble and I left ya at the movie show. And ya found out later your old man was killed durin' that time.

GINNY. I'll admit I wondered about that, but—

BRAD. Sure. Ya wondered— Then ya found out I had a record. Did time for knifin' a guy on the street. That made ya pretty certain, didn't it?

GINNY. (*Sighs helplessly*) Oh, Brad— If you'd only get that tremendous, colossal chip off your shoulder.

BRAD. Why? Gimme a reason to.

GINNY. (*Hesitates, then faces him squarely*) Because I believe in you. Because I—I love you, Brad.

BRAD. (*Looks at her longingly for a moment, then sweeps her into his arms*) Gee. Gee, Ginny. Honey—

GINNY. (*After a moment, still in his arms, looking up at him*) We're in this together now, aren't we?

BRAD. Uh-huh. Together.

GINNY. We'll fight it, darling. And we'll win.

BRAD. Yeah— (*Lets go of her and takes a step away.*) Yeah, maybe we'll win.

GINNY. We will. Listen— That gun you were carrying.

BRAD. What about it?

GINNY. When they check it, they'll find out, won't they? I mean, that it wasn't used to kill my father?

BRAD. (*Shrugs*) Sometimes it's pretty tough to tell two

bullets apart. When they been fired from guns of the same calibre.

GINNY. Is it?

BRAD. Yeah. If the barrel markin's happen to be pretty close— And those cops. They believe what they wanna believe.

GINNY. Don't say that.

BRAD. It's the truth. And I'm the guy can tell ya— Last time, after the knifin', they called it "unprovoked assault."

GINNY. Wasn't it?

BRAD. (*Looks at her*) Really wanna know?

GINNY. Yes, I really want to know. Everything about you, Brad. Things you felt you couldn't tell me before— How did it happen?

BRAD. (*After a moment*) I was riding along. Alone in my car. This other car pulled up alongside. Guys in it whoopin' and hollerin'. Y'know the kind?

GINNY. Uh-huh, I think so.

BRAD. They scraped my fender. Deliberately. I stopped and got out. Guess it made me pretty mad.

GINNY. It would anyone.

BRAD. The others piled out, too. There was some talk. Then this one guy—the leader—pulled a knife.

GINNY. Heavens!

BRAD. He came at me, and I got the knife away from him— (*Trying to control the emotions in that memory.*) Next thing I knew, he was stretched out on the pavement. Bleeding—

GINNY. (*Compassionately*) Oh, Brad—

BRAD. His friends got the cops. Way they told it, this other guy was arguin' peaceably and it was me pulled the knife. Claimed it was mine— And I could never prove it wasn't.

GINNY. It must've been terrible for you— Just terrible.

BRAD. (*Shrugs*) I managed.

GINNY. But Brad— How can you blame the police?

BRAD. What d'ya mean?

GINNY. All the witnesses were against you, weren't they?

BRAD. (*Nods*) Four of 'em. Nobody else saw it happen.

GINNY. Then how can you blame the police?

BRAD. I tried to tell 'em the truth, didn't I? That I was being framed— They wouldn't listen. All they were interested in was an arrest. And a conviction— 'Sall they ever care about.

GINNY. I can see now why you've been so bitter. But, Brad— After all, it was your word against four others. It's understandable why the police— You've got to make allowances.

BRAD. Why should I? Nobody ever made allowances for me.

GINNY. (*Looks at him*) Nobody?

BRAD. Nobody till now. (*Takes her in his arms again.*) Honey— Maybe I better tell ya why I been packin' that rod.

GINNY. If you want to.

BRAD. Yeah— Coupla weeks ago, I ran into one of those other guys. Friend of the one with the knife.

GINNY. One who'd been in the car with him?

BRAD. (*Nods*) Said his gang was out to even the score. Said they'd get me. Sometime when I was least expectin' it—

GINNY. (*Fearfully*) Oh, Brad!

BRAD. So I picked up that gun from a guy I know. For protection.

GINNY. I understand.

BRAD. But, Ginny—I'd never've used it. Not unless I absolutely had to. To save my own life— You believe that?

GINNY. Of course I do. I believed it before you ever told me. That's why I'm here like this now. (*Leans up and kisses him.*)

BRAD. (*Calls over to* JOE) All right, what do you want to know?

JOE. (*Walking over to join them*) Were you in the house at the time Hamlin was killed?

BRAD. No.

JOE. That's right. You and Miss Hamlin were together all evening. Forgot you told me.

BRAD. (*Exchanges glances with* GINNY) That—that's not exactly right.

JOE. Isn't?

BRAD. I left her for a while. At the show.

JOE. That right? Why?

BRAD. We had a mix-up.

GINNY. A silly quarrel, Sergeant. It didn't amount to anything.

JOE. Uh-huh.

GINNY. When I got out of the show a little later, Brad was waiting for me.

BRAD. By then I was over it. Bein' mad.

JOE. Know what time it was?

BRAD. Close to eleven, I guess.

JOE. (*To* GINNY) What time did the show let out?

GINNY. (*Considers*) About twenty minutes later. I'm sure it wasn't any longer than that.

JOE. Uh-huh. (*To* BRAD.) What'd you do in those twenty minutes?

BRAD. Nothin'. Just walked around gettin' over my temper.

JOE. Didn't go any particular place? Didn't run into anyone? No one saw you?

BRAD. (*Shrugs*) Not that I know of. I just walked the streets. It was pretty late. Nobody much around.

JOE. Yeah—

GINNY. He's telling you the truth now, Sergeant. You believe him, don't you?

JOE. I'd like to, Miss. But we'll have to check his story. Try to find someone who saw him wandering the streets.

GINNY. And if you can't?

JOE. (*Shrugs*) Then there's still the matter of that gun.

GINNY. About the gun— He had a reason for carrying it.

JOE. Uh-huh. I heard. Those threats you mentioned— You report 'em to your parole officer?

BRAD. (*Hesitates*) No.

JOE. Why not?

BRAD. What good would it have done? What good would the parole officer be to me if they jumped me some dark night?

NORA. (*Enters from Left, below the stairs*) Well— Got it settled yet?

JOE. No, ma'am. Not quite settled.

NORA. Think it's gonna take much longer?

JOE. (*Shrugs*) Hard to say.

NORA. Karl's death was bad enough. But all this probing. Digging down and disturbing the roots—I wish it was over.

JOE. I'm with you there, Mrs. Hamlin. But that's how it is when people kill. Roots are bound to get disturbed—

(*The DOORBELL rings, then* FRANK'S *voice is heard from off Right.*)

FRANK. (*Off Right*) Okay to come in?
NORA. Oh—yes, come in, Mr. Smith.

(FRANK *enters from Right. Stops inside arch.*)

JOE. They finish running that test, Frank?

FRANK. (*Nods*) Little while ago.

JOE. Got the results?

FRANK. Yeah. Right here. (*Gets a file card from his pocket.*)

JOE. (*Rises and crosses to him*) Can I see it?

(FRANK *hands him the card and he examines it while the others watch tensely.*)

Uh-huh—Guess that's it, Frank.

FRANK. (*Nods*) That's it.

JOE. Yeah— (*Sighs and comes down slowly.*) Okay, Roney. Looks like you're in the clear—

GINNY. Oh, Brad!

JOE. Tests show the murder bullet wasn't fired from your gun.

GINNY. Brad, I knew. I told you—

BRAD. (*Seems dazed*) Yeah— Yeah, honey, you told me.

JOE. Case it makes any difference, Roney, I wasn't much sold on you as a suspect anyway.

BRAD. You weren't?

JOE. (*Shakes his head*) Didn't seem to be any reason for your killing him. No motive.

GINNY. Of course there wasn't.

NORA. I'm glad, Brad. Glad you've been cleared.

BRAD. Thanks.

JOE. Not cleared of everything.

BRAD. What? I thought ya said—

JOE. Still that little question of the gun. Carrying concealed weapons.

BRAD. Yeah— Guess you'll hafta tell my parole officer.

JOE. (*Hesitates, then shakes his head*) You will.

BRAD. Me?

JOE. That's right. Tell him all the circumstances. 'Bout those threats. Tell him you bought the gun for protection. But you surrendered it to a police officer because— Because you thought better of it.

BRAD. (*Gratefully*) Yeah. Okay, I'll do that. Thanks. Thanks, Sergeant.

JOE. Take him into your confidence. Maybe he'll be able to suggest something. How to get those guys off your back. He's got ways, y'know.

BRAD. Uh-huh.

JOE. And maybe you'll find he *wants* to help you. Not just because it's his job. Maybe you'll even find out he's a human being just like you— If you'll give him a chance.

FRANK. And if you give yourself a chance, son. That's the important thing.

BRAD. I—

(*Turns away from them abruptly to mask his emotions, and crosses Down Left. GINNY goes to him and takes his hand. He looks at her and breaks into a slow smile.*)

FRANK. (*To* JOE) Well— Where's it leave us?

JOE. (*Shrugs*) 'Bout where we were before, I guess.

FRANK. Only worse.

JOE. How d'you figure that?

FRANK. We're about outta suspects.

JOE. Yeah.—(*Frowns in thought.*) Frank— Maybe we've been tackling this from the wrong end.

FRANK. How d'ya mean?

JOE. Instead of worrying about "Who"— Maybe we should concentrate on "how."

FRANK. Uh-huh.

JOE. How did Hamlin get behind that barricade, with his own gun—the wrong one—in his hand—dead?

FRANK. Sure must be an answer.

JOE. Gotta be.

FRANK. Only I can't think of one— Trouble is I'm not superstitious.

JOE. Superstitious?

FRANK. I don't believe in ghosts.

JOE. Ghost we're after is awfully live— Maybe we'd better talk some more to the one person we know was down here at the time.

NORA. You mean my mother, Mr. Friday?

JOE. Yes, ma'am.

NORA. Wish you didn't have to. You don't realize what a shock this whole thing has been to—

MRS. GAYLOR. (*From off Left on stairs*) Nonsense, Nora. You worry too much. (*Enters, slowly coming downstairs, the book under her arm.*)

NORA. Mother! Haven't you been asleep?

MRS. GAYLOR. Nope. (*She is at the foot of the stairs by now.*)
NORA. (*Goes to her and gives her a hand*) But those pills you took.
MRS. GAYLOR. I spit 'em out. Soon as you left my room.
NORA. (*Guiding her toward armchair Down Right*) Why?
MRS. GAYLOR. Wanted to hear what was goin' on. I'm interested— (*As she is passing* FRANK, *she drops the book.*)
FRANK. I'll get it. (*Starts to stoop for it.*)
MRS. GAYLOR. Needn't bother, young man. (*Quickly bends down and snatches it from his reach.*) Wish folks would quit treatin' me like an invalid— Almost makes me feel like one.

(JOE'S *eyes follow* MRS. GAYLOR.)

NORA. (*Seats* MRS. GAYLOR *in armchair*) Mother. Mean to say you've been listening all this time? Heard everything that went on?
MRS. GAYLOR. Most of it. When folks wasn't mumblin' in their beards. Ginny, I'm glad they set Brad loose.
GINNY. Me too, Grandma.
MRS. GAYLOR. Blind man could tell that boy's no killer.
BRAD. Thanks, Mrs. Gaylor.
MRS. GAYLOR. Don't thank me. I didn't do anything— Well, Mr. Friday. Fresh out of ideas, hey?
   (JOE *has been standing there in thought since the dropped book incident.*)
Mr. Friday.
JOE. What?
MRS. GAYLOR. Said you seemed to be fresh out of ideas.
JOE. Maybe. Will you let me see that book you have, Mrs. Gaylor?
   (*She sits there gaping at him; extends his hand for it.*)
Let me see it, please.

(Slowly she makes up her mind and hands it to him.) Thanks. *(Examines the cover.)* Frank— Take a look at this. *(Gives him the book.)*

FRANK. *(Glances at it; then deadpan)* Uh-huh— A slug. Embedded in the cover.

JOE. Yeah.

GINNY. *(Aghast)* Oh, no! No—not Grandma—

NORA. Mother. Does this mean that *you*—that you—?

JOE. *(Gently)* Want to tell us about it, Mrs. Gaylor?

NORA. *(Going on in a dull voice)* She never told me, but I—I suppose I guessed. When that second shot became so important—I heard it, of course.

JOE. You did.

NORA. And I knew Mother was the only one down here with Karl at the time—I suppose I guessed.

JOE. *(To* MRS. GAYLOR*)* Where's the pistol, ma'am?

(She has been sitting with her chin on her chest; now she looks up at him.)

What'd you do with the pistol, Mrs. Gaylor?

MRS. GAYLOR. I'll get it for you. *(Rises and slowly crosses to fireplace; reaches up inside and gets an automatic.)*

JOE. *(Crosses to her and she hands him the pistol)* Thanks. *(Examines it; unloading it and sniffing at the barrel.)*

MRS. GAYLOR. *(At same time)* Kept it hangin' on the damper hook. Didn't think anyone'd look for it there—

FRANK. *(To* JOE*)* Three-eighty?

JOE. Yeah.

MRS. GAYLOR. *(Sitting in upstage loveseat)* Belonged to my husband. He got it when he was overseas in the war—first war. Nora never knew I kept it.

JOE. Uh-huh.

MRS. GAYLOR. Then when Mr. Hamlin started comin' round, makin' all those threats—I got worried. For Nora. Dug that pistol out of an old trunk where I had it. Hung it up there in the fireplace— Just in case, you know.

JOE. Yes, ma'am. About last night. Wanta tell us about that?

MRS. GAYLOR. (*Hesitates*) If I did— If I told you what happened, Mr. Friday, you'd never believe it.

JOE. Whyn't you try us?

MRS. GAYLOR. All right— After Nora went upstairs, I was sittin' in that chair. Reading. Like I told you, he started cursing at me.

JOE. Yes, ma'am.

MRS. GAYLOR. Paid him no heed at first. Told him to go away. That Nora was finished with him— He wouldn't go.

JOE. Uh-huh.

MRS. GAYLOR. All of a sudden, he pulled his gun out and started waving it around. Said if Nora didn't come back to him, he'd—he'd kill himself. I thought it was just some more of his play acting.

JOE. Yes, ma'am.

MRS. GAYLOR. Figured if I ignored him, he'd go away. So I went back to the book. That only made him madder than ever.

JOE. That right?

MRS. GAYLOR. He grabbed the book. Right out of my hand, mind you, and—and shot it. Then he threw it into the fireplace.

JOE. I see.

MRS. GAYLOR. I went to the fireplace to get it. And then— Just all of a sudden something came over me—I don't think I've ever been so mad in all my life. Furious, blind mad—I got the gun off the hook and I turned and I—I shot him.

(*The* OTHERS *are watching very quietly.* NORA *is silently crying.*)

That look on his face— So surprised and scared and— He turned and ran into the study. Locked the door behind him. Then I heard him moving something up to it.

FRANK. The chair.

Mrs. Gaylor. Right after that, I heard him falling— Then Nora came downstairs.

Nora. Why didn't you tell me, Mother?

Mrs. Gaylor. Wasn't any reason to. I had to think about it. What I'd done— And what I had to do. 'Course, if they started to arrest someone else for it, I knew I'd have to give myself up. But I thought maybe it wouldn't come to that— You believe me, Mr. Friday?

Joe. Sure.

Mrs. Gaylor. One thing I guess I ought to tell you.

Joe. What's that?

Mrs. Gaylor. That gun. It's got an awfully easy trigger. Don't have to pull it very hard to make it go off. Maybe it was an accident. I don't know. I'm sure I really did it on purpose. But I guess that doesn't make any difference—

Joe. (*Gently*) You'll have to come downtown with us, Mrs. Gaylor. Wanta get ready?

Mrs. Gaylor. Yes, sir. (*Rises.*) Yes, sir. I'll do it right away.

Nora. Ginny, will you give Grandma a hand?

Ginny. Of course. (*Goes to her.*) C'mon, Grandma. I'll help you.

Mrs. Gaylor. (*As* Ginny *guides her out and up the stairs*) Thanks, dear— It was so easy. Never knew before how easy— Just pulling a little trigger. Without even wanting to, maybe. And a man's dead. Gone for good— So easy to do. (*They are off.*)

Nora. (*To* Joe) Will Mother have to— Is it going to be all right?

Joe. We don't decide that, Mrs. Hamlin.

Nora. But she told the truth. Everything you wanted to know. Isn't that going to make a difference?

Joe. We'll put it down that way. On our report.

Frank. 'Bout all we *can* do, ma'am.

Nora. Well— Thank you.

Frank. But that story of hers— (*Shakes his head.*) Still pretty hard to believe.

ACT III   DRAGNET   77

JOE. I don't know, Frank. Way she is, it could happen.
FRANK. Yeah. Guess so.
JOE. Shooting up her book like that. (*Looks at the book.*) Might make her mad enough to kill him.
BRAD. What's the title of the book, Sergeant?
JOE. The Holy Bible.

BLACKOUT

ACT THREE

SCENE 2

THE TIME: *About a month later; late evening.*

THE PLACE: *The office at Police Headquarters.*

AT RISE: *The LIGHTS are on in the office area; off in the living room area. FRANK is discovered seated behind the desk, talking into the phone. There are two coffee containers on the desk; FRANK drinks from one of them as he carries on the phone conversation.*

FRANK. (*Into phone*) Uh-huh— Yeah— Sure, Fay— Nope, been awful quiet tonight. So far— Yeah— Okay, Fay, I'll tell him— No, he stepped outta the office a minute— Uh-huh— Yeah— Yeah—
    (JOE *enters.* FRANK *looks up and cups a hand over the mouthpiece; to* JOE.)
Fay.
JOE. Uh-huh. (*Crosses and sits Right of desk.*)
FRANK. (*Into phone*) Yeah— Yeah— Aw, no— Fay, will ya cut it out?—Course I'll be careful. It's just a job, like any other— Always have so far, haven't I?—Yeah— Yeah, I'll call ya— So long. (*Hangs up; looks embarrassedly at* JOE.) Women. Always worryin'.

Joe. Uh-huh.

Frank. Guess they can't help themselves. Way they're built.

Joe. Yeah. (*Reaches for the other container.*) This my coffee?

Frank. (*Nods*) That's it.

Joe. Thanks. Sixteen cents, wasn't it? (*Reaches in his pocket for change.*)

Frank. Right.

Joe. (*Gets out some change and hands it to* Frank) Don't seem to have the odd penny. Have to owe it to you.

Frank. I'll mark it down in my book.

Joe. No joke. Pennies can add up.

Frank. (*Nods*) Found that out since Fay and I've been hitched.

Joe. Oh— (*Gets a slip of paper from his pocket.*) Remember the Hamlin case, Frank?

Frank. Hamlin? Oh, sure. 'Bout a month ago. Old lady got mad at her son-in-law for shootin' up her Bible and killed him.

Joe. (*Nods*) That's the one— Got the report here on the final disposition of the case.

Frank. How'd it go?

Joe. (*Reads from paper*) "—Jessie Margaret Gaylor was examined by three psychiatrists appointed by the court and found to be insane during the commission of the crime—"

Frank. Uh-huh.

Joe. (*Reads*) "A sanity hearing was held and she was made a ward of the state and placed in the State Hospital at Mendocino for treatment."

Frank. Yeah. Guess that figured.

Joe. (*Nods*) Be better off that way— Maybe at Mendocino she can catch up on her sleep.

Frank. Hope so. Oh, Joe. Fay's been after me again. Wants to know if you're mad at her.

Joe. Why?

FRANK. Haven't been out to the house like ya promised. For a feed.

JOE. Any time you say, Frank.

FRANK. Tomorrow okay?

JOE. Sure.

FRANK. I'll tell her to get another roast. Last one went pretty bad from settin' around in the refrigerator.

JOE. Tough. Have to throw it out?

FRANK. Nope. Ate it anyway. Couldn't afford not to—

(*The PHONE rings.*)

JOE. (*Picks it up and answers it*) Homicide, Friday— Yeah— Oh, yeah, Mrs. Hamlin— Sure I remember. Hope it's gonna work out all right for your mother— Yeah— What?—Well, congratulations— Uh-huh— Uh-huh— Just a minute, I'll ask him. (*Cups hand over the mouthpiece.*) Feel like going to a wedding next Sunday?

FRANK. Huh? Who's gettin' married?

JOE. Whole flock of people. It's a double wedding: Ginny Hamlin and Brad Roney; and Mrs. Hamlin and Walter Markov— Wanta go?

FRANK. Sure. Guess I can make it.

JOE. (*Into phone*) Said he'd be delighted, Mrs. Hamlin— Uh-huh— Yeah, Sunday at eleven. We'll be there— Okay, and thanks for the invitation— G'bye. (*Hangs up.*) Well— Looks like they've got their problems solved.

FRANK. Uh-huh. That marriage idea, Joe. It's a great problem solver.

JOE. Seems to be.

(*The PHONE rings.*)

FRANK. I'll get it. (*Picks up phone and answers it.*) Homicide, Smith— Yeah— Uh-huh— Right— (*Makes note on pad.*) Melrose and Vine— Uh-huh— Yeah, we'll be right over— Okay. (*Hangs up.*)

JOE. What've you got, Frank?

FRANK. Coupla hoods shot up a liquor store— Proprietor badly wounded.

JOE. Guess we'd better hustle on down there.

FRANK. Yeah.

(They gulp down their coffee, then stand up and get their hats.)

Hope Fay wasn't listenin' to the police calls. She'll worry.

JOE. Uh-huh.

FRANK. *(As they cross to exit)* Keep tellin' her there's no reason to, but she won't listen. It's just a job, I tell her. Like any other. Isn't that right, Joe?

JOE. Sure. That's what it is, Frank— Just a job.

(They exit and the LIGHTS slowly dim on an empty stage.)

END OF PLAY

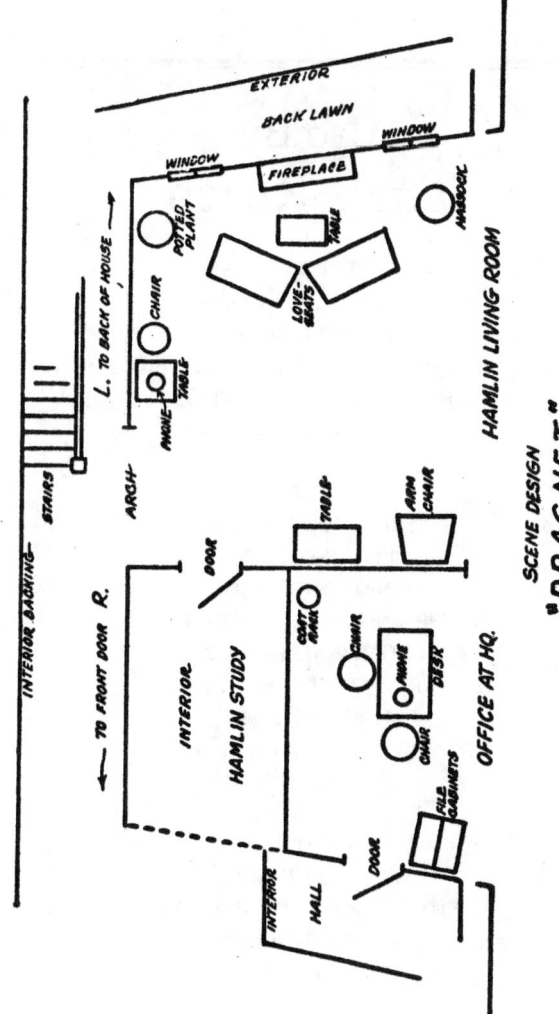

Also By
James Reach

AFRAID OF THE DARK
ARE TEACHERS HUMAN?
BEAR WITNESS
THE CASE OF THE LAUGHING DWARF
THE CLOCK STRUCK TWELVE
DAVID AND LISA
DRAGNET
FOR THE DEFENSE
THE INNOCENT ONE
LEADING LADY
LUNATICS AT LARGE
MR. SNOOP IS MURDERED
MURDER IS MY BUSINESS
MURDER TAKES THE STAGE
MY FRIEND IRMA
NOW THAT APRIL'S HERE
ONE MAD NIGHT
PATTERNS
QUICK TRICKS
WE'RE ALL GUILTY
WHY NOT JOIN THE GIRAFFES
WOMEN IN WHITE
YOU, THE JURY

SAMUELFRENCH.COM

OTHER TITLES AVAILABLE FROM SAMUEL FRENCH

MURDER AMONG FRIENDS
Bob Barry

Comedy thriller / 4m, 2f / Interior
Take an aging, exceedingly vain actor; his very rich wife; a double dealing, double loving agent, plunk them down in an elegant New York duplex and add dialogue crackling with wit and laughs, and you have the basic elements for an evening of pure, sophisticated entertainment. Angela, the wife and Ted, the agent, are lovers and plan to murder Palmer, the actor, during a contrived robbery on New Year's Eve. But actor and agent are also lovers and have an identical plan to do in the wife. A murder occurs, but not one of the planned ones.

"Clever, amusing, and very surprising."
– *New York Times*

"A slick, sophisticated show that is modern and very funny."
– WABC TV

SAMUELFRENCH.COM

www.ingramcontent.com/pod-product-compliance
Lightning Source LLC
Chambersburg PA
CBHW070647300426
44111CB00013B/2307